Christian Heroes: Then & Now

LOTTIE MOON

Giving Her All for China

Christian Heroes: Then & Now

LOTTIE MOON

Giving Her All for China

JANET & GEOFF BENGE

YWAM Publishing is the publishing ministry of Youth With A Mission (YWAM), an international missionary organization of Christians from many denominations dedicated to presenting Jesus Christ to this generation. To this end, YWAM has focused its efforts in three main areas: (1) training and equipping believers for their part in fulfilling the Great Commission (Matthew 28:19), (2) personal evangelism, and (3) mercy ministry (medical and relief work).

To learn more about our books and materials, call (425) 771-1153 or (800) 922-2143 or email books@ywampublishing.com. Visit us online at www.ywampublishing.com.

Lottie Moon: Giving Her All for China

Published by YWAM Publishing
a ministry of Youth With A Mission
P.O. Box 55787, Seattle, WA 98155-0787

ISBN 978-1-57658-188-9 (paperback)
ISBN 978-1-57658-595-5 (e-book)

Eighth printing 2025

Printed in the United States of America

CHRISTIAN HEROES: THEN & NOW

Adoniram Judson
Albert Schweitzer
Amy Carmichael
Betty Greene
Brother Andrew
Cameron Townsend
Charles Mulli
Clarence Jones
Corrie ten Boom
Count Zinzendorf
C. S. Lewis
C. T. Studd
David Bussau
David Livingstone
Dietrich Bonhoeffer
D. L. Moody
Elisabeth Elliot
Eric Liddell
Florence Young
Francis Asbury
George Müller
Gladys Aylward
Helen Roseveare
Hudson Taylor
Ida Scudder
Isobel Kuhn
Jacob DeShazer
Jim Elliot
John Flynn
John Newton
John Wesley
John Williams
Jonathan Goforth
Klaus-Dieter John
Lillian Trasher
Loren Cunningham
Lottie Moon
Mary Slessor
Mildred Cable
Nate Saint
Norman Grubb
Paul Brand
Rachel Saint
Richard Wurmbrand
Rowland Bingham
Samuel Zwemer
Sundar Singh
Wilfred Grenfell
William Booth
William Carey

Available in paperback, e-book, and audiobook formats. Unit study curriculum guides are available for select biographies.

www.YWAMpublishing.com

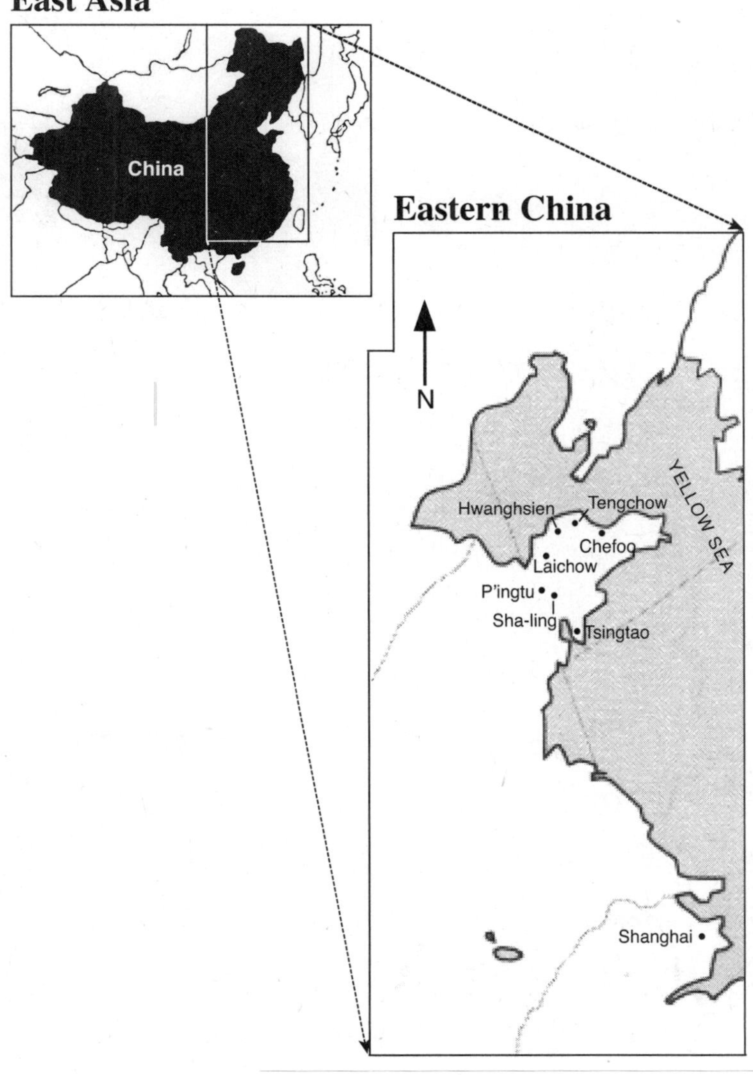
East Asia
China
Eastern China
N
YELLOW SEA
Hwanghsien
Tengchow
Chefoo
Laichow
P'ingtu
Sha-ling
Tsingtao
Shanghai

Contents

Chapter 1

Viewmont

Six-year-old Lottie Moon sat up straight in her front-row pew, barely daring to turn her head. She knew it would make her black ringlets bob, and that would attract attention. The silk sash on her pinafore was tied too tightly, and she cautiously took some extra deep breaths in a vain attempt to loosen it. Her starched collar pricked the back of her neck. She stopped short of scratching her neck, since that would be very bad manners. No, she would just have to sit still and endure the discomfort.

Lottie knew all about church manners because she was in church so often. The pastor was a circuit-riding preacher, and he stopped off at Scottsville on either Saturday or Sunday to hold a service. Even when the service was on a Saturday,

Lottie still attended Sunday school. She had little choice about this, since her father, Edward Moon, practically ran the church. He had started the Sunday school and was both a deacon and the church clerk. He also often represented the church at various Baptist Association meetings.

Like most children, Lottie would have rather been outside on such a beautiful spring morning. The peach blossoms were in bloom, and the crickets were chirping. Indeed, Lottie could hear the crickets outside over the sound of the pastor's voice.

The mention of her grandmother's name focused Lottie's attention back on what the pastor was saying. "Let us take a moment to honor the memory of Sarah Coleman Turner Barclay Harris, esteemed and tireless worker for the Lord, who departed life this last Wednesday, May 5, 1847," he said.

Lottie counted her grandmother's names carefully as the pastor said them. He had it right; there were five of them. She had asked her mother only the night before to explain how her grandmother came to have so many names. According to her mother, Lottie's grandmother was known as Sarah Coleman Turner when she was a little girl, just as Lottie herself was really Charlotte Digges Moon. As a young woman, Lottie's grandmother had married Robert Barclay, who was Lottie's mother's father. Soon after Lottie's mother was born, her father drowned. After the death of her husband, Lottie's grandmother had traveled to Virginia and married Captain John Harris.

Captain Harris had been the richest man in Albemarle County by far. He owned over three thousand acres of land consisting of ten different tobacco and cotton plantations that were worked by eight hundred slaves. He also made regular trips to New Orleans and Kentucky to conduct business. When Captain Harris died in 1832, several years before Lottie was born, the largest of his plantations, Viewmont, was left to Lottie's grandmother. And now that she was dead, it belonged to Lottie's mother and father.

As far as Lottie was able to think it through, her grandmother's death would not change much in her life. After all, the Moon family had lived at Viewmont from the time her parents were married. However, Lottie did think life around the plantation would be a lot less boring without her grandmother around trying to get Lottie to remember all the ins and outs of her family's history. There was just too much to remember. Lottie's great-grandfather, Thomas Barclay, had been a friend of Thomas Jefferson. He also had been dispatched by George Washington to be the first U.S. ambassador to France and Morocco. Lottie's uncle, Dr. James Barclay, now owned the old Jefferson homestead that was named Monticello. There was also the Moon side of the family, and more cousins than she could remember, some of them related on both her mother's and her father's sides of the family. "Double cousins" her grandmother had always called them when she tried to explain the family tree.

Lottie continued listening to the pastor. "We all owe much to Mrs. Sarah Harris," he said. "She has been a generous supporter and benefactor of the Scottsville Baptist Church since its timely establishment over six years ago. I am sure many of you have read in the *Baptist Press* that Mrs. Harris has made a munificent provision for us, even in her untimely death."

The big words the pastor was using made Lottie's head spin as she tried to understand what he was saying. She guessed he was talking about the one hundred dollars her grandmother had given the church in her will. That was a large sum of money to most people, but Lottie had an idea it wasn't really that much to anyone in her family. She was old enough to have figured out that when it came to material things, she could have just about anything she wanted. She looked along the pew she was seated on. Beside her sat her oldest brother, fifteen-year-old Tom. He already had a fine gilded stallion of his own and a trap, a light two-wheeled carriage with springs, to go with it. Next to Tom sat thirteen-year-old Orianna, or Orie, as the family called her. She loved to read, and their father had bought her an entire library of books, some of them in Latin and Greek, so Orianna could read whenever she wanted to. Isaac, or Ike, Lottie's other brother, was two years younger than Orie, but he wasn't interested in reading at all. Instead, Mr. Moon had bought him a fine hunting bow.

Lottie sighed quietly as she thought about her three older siblings. They were all a bit too grown-up for her liking. All she wanted was someone who would play with her. Once Orianna had whispered to Lottie that their mother had given birth to three other children, but they had all died when they were very young. However, Lottie did have one little sister, Colie. Colie's real name was Sarah Coleman Moon, after their grandmother, but for some reason the nickname Colie had stuck. Colie was only three years old, and Mamie, one of the household servants, looked after her, though with strict instructions from Mrs. Moon not to let the child out of her sight. To Lottie's dismay, Colie wasn't big enough to run through the cotton fields with her, climb the peach trees, or play in the packing shed, even if she could have escaped Mamie's watchful eyes. Colie wasn't even old enough to sit still in church, and she stayed home in the nursery while the rest of the family attended. Of course, this made Lottie feel very grown-up.

When the church service was over, the congregation spilled out into the warm spring morning. Lottie teamed up with some of her young cousins, and they played together as they walked down the stone path that led to the dusty road in front of the church.

Finally Lottie's mother, Anna Maria Moon, bustled Lottie and Ike toward the family's carriage. "It's time to go now," she said firmly.

Lottie, who was halfway through telling her cousin James about how a pair of sparrows had nested in the hedge beside the kitchen, wanted to stay and finish her story, but she knew better than to argue with her mother. Mrs. Moon may have been only four and a half feet tall, but when she gave an order, everyone—even Lottie's father—paid attention.

Finally Lottie scrambled up the steps of the carriage and scooted along the leather seat until she had positioned herself by the far window. With great relief she gave her sash a big tug, allowing her to breathe freely for the first time all morning. Jesse the coachman clicked the reins, and they were off on the nine-mile trip back home to Viewmont. Lottie stuck her head out the window as far as it would go. She loved the scent of the peach and apple blossoms and the sight of the newly planted rows of cotton. The distant hills, which Orie had told her were the foothills of the Blue Ridge Mountains, reminded Lottie of folds of green velvet, like the fabric of her mother's best dress.

Lottie knew the exact fence post that marked the beginning of the fifteen-hundred-acre Viewmont plantation. Even though she was too young to be taught by the tutors who came to the house to instruct the older children in the classics, French, and music, Lottie had learned some of the history of the plantation from her father, who had told her that Viewmont was one of the oldest plantations in Albemarle County. Joshua Fry, a fellow surveyor and friend of George Washington, had built the first house on the property in 1744. Later he had sold the place to Edmund Randolph, a governor of Virginia. When the first house burned down, a more modern one was built to replace it. That was the house the Moon family now lived in. Lottie loved the house, especially the secret stairway located behind a fake wall in the fireplace. It made the house feel mysterious, and Lottie loved a good mystery.

As the carriage rounded the last turn in the road and the house came into view, Lottie watched as Shep, the family's faithful collie dog, bounded out to meet them. The two huge brick chimneys of the house always looked odd to Lottie without smoke billowing from them, but the Moons had strict rules about the Sabbath. Every Saturday Juju the cook fried chicken and baked ham while Mrs. Moon made pies and biscuits. Between them, they prepared enough food for two days so that no fires would have to be lit and nothing would have to be cooked on Sunday. Instead, Sunday was for reading the Bible and other Christian books as well as resting and discussing "uplifting and fitting" matters. Normally Lottie found this practice a bit of a trial. For one thing, she did not like cold day-old biscuits, not to mention cold fried chicken. Still, today she didn't mind. Her mother was halfway through reading Lottie the story of America's first female missionary, Ann Judson. They were right at the part where the Judsons were being pursued by the British authorities in India. That was an adventure, and Lottie was quite happy to endure cold biscuits and chicken in order to hear the end of the story.

Lottie had imagined that not much would change after the death of her grandmother, but she had been wrong. Her father, who up until then had been a merchant, took over the day-to-day running of the plantation, something her grandmother had done until the time of her death. His new responsibilities now meant that he made fewer trips to the large port cities on the coast, and Lottie thus got to see much more of him, which made her very happy.

Her mother's brother, Dr. James Barclay, also plotted a career change now that his mother was not around to tell him what to do. He owned a successful pharmacy, but as the years went by, he spent more time preaching at the Disciples of Christ church and less time selling medicines.

When Lottie was ten years old, her cousin Sarah Barclay told her the most extraordinary news. The two of them were sitting together on the back stoop, picking over some black-eyed peas for dinner, when Sarah blurted out, "Lottie, can you keep a secret? I know Papa wants to tell your mother first, but I will simply burst if I don't tell someone!"

Lottie put down the bowl she was holding. "Of course. What's the matter?" she asked, surprised to see her cousin so animated.

Sarah lowered her voice. "Yesterday afternoon, around three o'clock, Papa came home from doctoring old Mr. Boardman down the road who has consumption. Anyway, I was sitting in the yard memorizing a poem, the boys were building a treehouse nearby, while Mother was sitting on the veranda reading her Bible. When Papa arrived, he got off his horse and yelled to us all. 'Come here. I have something I want to tell you.' Of course we all gathered around Papa."

"Well, what did he want to tell you?" interjected Lottie, unable to think of anything important enough to excite Sarah this much.

"Well," Sarah went on, "he began reading to us from the Bible, and when he was finished, he talked about how Christians should take the gospel to those who have not heard it."

"And?" quizzed Lottie impatiently.

"And then he told us he wanted to go to Jerusalem to be a missionary to the Jewish people."

There was silence for a moment.

"Well, what do you think of that?" Sarah finally asked.

"Is he serious? Would it be soon?" Lottie replied, her thoughts in a jumble.

"Very soon," replied Sarah. "Papa wants us all to go with him! He asked each of us to think about it last night, and if we wanted to go with him to sign our names in the family Bible this morning."

Lottie could hardly believe what she was hearing. "And did you?" she asked.

Sarah nodded, her eyes shining. "Every one of us signed. Papa says we will leave within a month."

Lottie gasped. When she had been younger, six and seven and eight years old, she had believed everything her parents and the pastor told her about God and the Bible, but now that she was ten, most of it didn't make sense anymore. Even though the Moons tried not to talk about religious differences in front of the children, Lottie was a smart young girl who knew that many churchgoers in Scottsville and nearby Charlottesville avoided one another because of their different views on religion. Her own Uncle James and Aunt Julia were a case in point. They had left the Baptist church to join a new denomination called the Disciples of Christ. And they weren't the only ones; entire congregations had left the Baptist church to join this new denomination. Bitterness and gossip ran deep, and Lottie, following the lead of her older sister, Orie, decided she wanted nothing at all to do with religion or God.

And now her three cousins were going off to the other side of the world to teach Jews about Jesus Christ. Lottie attempted a weak smile, but inside she could hardly believe that Uncle James would drag his family away from their comfortable and happy home. But the thing that troubled Lottie the most was that Sarah and the rest of her family seemed to think going to Jerusalem was a good idea.

What could she say? In the end, Lottie grasped Sarah's hand. "You will write to me, won't you?" she said, certain that they would be leaving soon. Uncle James was the kind of man who, when he announced something, went right out and did it.

Sure enough, a month later, people from all over the district gathered in Scottsville for a farewell service for the Barclays. Two of the Moon children were not in attendance. Tom, Lottie's now nineteen-year-old brother, was in Charlottesville studying to be a doctor, and Mollie, the newest Moon baby, was at home with her nanny.

Lottie wished she could have stayed home, too. The thought of her cousins leaving Virginia, possibly forever, made her very sad, especially since they were going off to be missionaries. If there was a single way to waste a life, Lottie told herself, being a missionary was it.

Chapter 2

Proper Young Ladies

Lottie watched out the window as her father's carriage was brought around to the front entrance of Viewmont. It seemed to her these days that someone was always coming or going. It was 1853, and thirteen-year-old Lottie was the oldest child left at home. Tom was in his final year at medical school, and Ike was in his first year at the University of Virginia studying to become a lawyer. Meanwhile, Orie was attending Troy Female Seminary, where she was learning all sorts of interesting facts about the new women's rights movement. In fact, some of her teachers had been at Seneca Falls in 1848 for the first Women's Rights Convention, and Elizabeth Blackwell and Lucretia Mott had come to Troy Female Seminary to visit the teachers.

"So you will make sure the new driveway is dug out to a depth of at least ten inches before the stones are laid on top." Lottie heard her father instructing her mother as the two walked down the spiral staircase together.

"Yes, Edward, I'll see to that," replied her mother. "And I have the instructions written down on how to have the crape myrtles trimmed. I'm hoping they'll bloom well this year."

Lottie watched as her parents stopped at the bottom of the stairs and chatted about the last few matters her mother would need to take care of while her father was away in New Orleans on business. As they talked, Lottie's newest sister, twenty-two-month-old Robinette, played quietly at her father's feet.

Edward Moon looked out the window. "I'm glad to see the snow's stopped," he said, and then turning to the butler, he asked, "Louis, has my wooden trunk been placed in the carriage yet?"

"Yes, master," replied the old slave, bowing slightly. "I put it there myself."

"Good," Mr. Moon said, and then turning to his family, he continued, "I will see you all when I get back."

"Good-bye, dear," said his wife. "Take care. This is not a good season to be traveling."

Edward Moon laughed and rustled Lottie's braids. "Your mother is a worrier!" he exclaimed. "I expect to hear your French verbs when I get home, young lady."

"Yes, Papa," responded Lottie, relieved that he hadn't asked to see her geometry calculations. French verbs were easy compared to the properties of a circle.

Lottie felt a blast of cold air as Louis opened the front door and escorted her father to the carriage. She shivered and then lifted Robinette up so they could watch the carriage head off down the tree-lined drive and disappear around the bend.

Six days later an envelope edged in black arrived at Viewmont. Lottie watched as her mother opened it with trembling hands and then burst into deep sobs. It was quite a while before her mother was able to read the letter to her. According to the account in the letter, on January 26, her father had been aboard the steamboat *James Robb* when a fire broke out. The steamboat was very close to shore, and the passengers began jumping overboard and wading ashore. Edward Moon had dragged his wooden chest, which contained the gold coins he was taking to New Orleans, across the deck and then jumped into the freezing water. With considerable effort he had hoisted the trunk onto his back and carried it ashore. Once ashore he collapsed in the mud, and when the other passengers tried to rouse him, they discovered he was dead. He had died of either a stroke or heart failure; no one could be sure which. The letter ended by saying his body would be delivered to Viewmont the next day.

The weeks that followed the arrival of the letter were a blur to Lottie. Hundreds of people came to the house to pay their respects; there was a huge funeral service at the Scottsville Baptist Church and a smaller one at the graveside in Viewmont. Afterward Lottie hated to look out the parlor window and see the black soil around the newly dug grave in the family cemetery.

Lottie's mother was overcome with grief at the turn of events. She insisted that Robinette's name be changed to "Edmonia Harris Moon" as a way to honor her husband. Gradually the family returned to some sort of order, but it was never the same without Lottie's father around.

Edward Moon had left behind a very specific will in which he wrote that all of his children—even the girls—were to have as much education as they wanted. And when Mrs. Moon died, everything in the estate was to be split equally among all the children.

Lottie was grateful that her father had made arrangements for her to go to college. This was an unusual step, and many of the neighbors thought it was scandalous to waste money on sending girls to college. Most southern girls did not even have a high school education; their "job" was to be pretty and polite so that they could attract a good husband. Once they were married, their time was to be taken up raising children, offering hospitality, and managing the house. All the women in Lottie's family had followed this pattern, and while Lottie was not opposed to doing the same herself, she was glad for the choice her father had given her.

By the fall of 1854, Lottie was ready to spread her wings, and she left home to attend the Virginia Female Seminary as a boarder. By now her brother Tom was a fully qualified doctor and had married a wealthy and "suitable" young belle named Helen Vaughan Wilson. After their wedding they had decided to stay on at Viewmont to help Mrs. Moon manage the huge plantation.

Orianna was off again, too, this time to Pennsylvania to enroll at the Quaker-run Pennsylvania Female Medical School. The school, Orie told Lottie proudly, was only four years old, and no southerner had lasted more than a few months at it. Orie fully intended to be the first southern woman to graduate as a doctor from the school.

The two sisters promised to write to each other regularly, and that is what they did. Lottie would write letters telling Orie all about the Latin texts she was busy reading, while Orie's letters were filled with startling new ideas about freedom. Many members of the faculty at the medical school were Quakers, who were committed to freeing slaves. Some of them were even links in the Underground Railway, which helped runaway slaves make it to freedom in the northern states. Not only that, the Pennsylvania Female Medical School was a hotbed of "freethinking" women who were calling for women to be treated equally with men. Dr. Ann Preston, Orie's anatomy teacher, was a close friend of Lucretia Mott, one of the women at the forefront of the Seneca Falls Convention, and she often led discussions about women's rights in American society. She even thought women should have the right to vote!

The women at the medical school faced stiff opposition from the otherwise all-male medical profession. Orie wrote how the female interns were forbidden to treat patients in public hospitals, so the school had opened its own clinic to treat only women. It was the first such clinic in the country to do so.

The year sped by, and the two sisters were together again at Viewmont for the summer. By now both of them refused to attend church with their mother and instead spent the hours together discussing the plight of women's rights in America.

Lottie went back to Virginia Female Seminary in the fall of 1855 along with her younger sister Colie, who was about to start her schooling there as well. It was hard to leave behind little Edmonia, or Eddie, as she had come to be called. Eddie was four years old now, and Lottie loved to play with her. There was another baby in the house, too: Thomas Moon, her brother Tom and his wife Helen's first child. However, they wouldn't be staying on much longer at Viewmont. As soon as Helen was strong enough, Tom told Lottie, the three of them were going to head down the Missouri River on their way west to join the Californian gold rush. Ike, who had recently been admitted as a lawyer to the Albemarle Bar, came home to take over Tom's responsibilities running the plantation.

Lottie had been back at the Virginia Female Seminary only a few weeks when she received the terrible news. Tom and Helen and baby Thomas had been on a riverboat just west of Leavenworth, Kansas, when an epidemic of cholera had broken out onboard. Since none of the three of them were sick, Tom had taken his wife and baby son ashore and found them a boardinghouse to stay in. Since he was a doctor, Tom had gone back onboard the riverboat to care for the sick. Within days he had contracted cholera himself and soon died. Lottie was stunned by the news. Tom was only twenty-three years old. It seemed unbelievable to her that she would never see him again.

In an attempt to forget her sorrow, Lottie plunged into her studies. She did very well in Latin and French, but no matter how hard she tried, she only scraped through in mathematics.

Little in the way of "proper" entertainment was available to the girls at the school, which over the summer had changed its name to Hollins Institute. The students were given only two hours of "uncommitted" time a day. The rest of their time was taken up with a schedule of study, meals, and endless hours in chapel. Indeed, about the most exciting thing at the school was the trip across the street to Enon Baptist Church on Sundays. Not that Lottie ever listened to the sermon. No. She sat with her cousin Cary Ann Coleman, and they whispered gossip to each other about the young men in the congregation.

All the structure associated with school was difficult for Lottie. As a child she had been schooled at home and had had a lot of freedom to romp and play. But now, at fourteen, she was supposed to be a young lady. Lottie told herself she simply wasn't yet ready to give up having fun. She would often lie awake at night thinking up practical jokes to play on her friends and even on the teachers.

On the eve of April Fools' Day 1856, while Cary Ann drifted off to sleep, Lottie was thinking very hard about something spectacular to do, something that everyone would be aware of. Suddenly it came to her. What was the thing she hated most about Hollins Institute? The schedule! And what kept everyone on schedule? The bells that rang every fifteen minutes from the school bell tower. Lottie's mind raced, and she had to hold her hand over her mouth to suppress a giggle, her plan was so good. She just had to make sure she woke up very early the next morning, preferably before dawn.

A few hours later, Lottie was wide-awake. The sun was not yet up, and the only light that shone in through the leaded window of her room was from the moon. Lottie slipped out of bed and into her coat and slippers. She then rolled her blankets into a bundle, and very carefully, without making a sound, she crept across the wooden floor and opened the door into the hallway. She looked back to see whether Cary Ann would stir. She didn't. Lottie tiptoed upstairs and removed the brass key from where it hung on a peg beside the attic door.

As quietly as possible she fit the key in the lock, turned it, and swung the huge oak door open.

Lottie closed the door carefully behind her and stood for a moment while her eyes adjusted to the dim light. After a minute or two, she could make out a pile of old desks and bed frames in the far corner and several trunks lined up against the wall. Then she saw what she was looking for—the ladder up to the rafters and then, higher still, another ladder that led to the belfry. Lottie took a deep breath and wrapped her coat belt around the blanket roll and then tied it around her waist. Step by step she began to climb the ladder to the rafters. As she climbed, Lottie thought about how most of the girls in her class would be afraid to do what she was doing—but not Lottie. She had climbed a thousand trees at Viewmont, and when she was younger, she and Ike had played hide-and-seek, scrambling over the huge bales of cotton in the packing shed.

When Lottie reached the top of the ladder, she climbed out onto the rafters and, balancing carefully, made her way over to the next ladder. This one took her higher still, right into the belfry tower itself. Lottie could see the ropes hanging down through the rafters to the floor below. She could just imagine the school caretaker pulling those ropes in an hour, at 6 A.M., as he did each morning.

"But they won't work this morning, April Fool!" Lottie laughed to herself as she carefully untied the blanket roll and draped blankets over the clapper of the large brass bell. She then tied the corners of the blankets to one of the ropes to hold them in place.

When she was satisfied she had completely muffled any sound the bell might make, Lottie climbed down the ladder and scrambled across the rafters and down the second ladder to the attic floor. Wiping cobwebs off her, she opened the attic door, locked it behind her, and replaced the key on the peg before slipping back downstairs to her room. Thankfully Cary Ann was still sleeping peacefully as Lottie took off her coat and slippers and lay down on her bed.

Lottie lay still straining to hear what might happen next. She watched as the sun peeked through the window and cast its light on the far wall. Lottie knew it was long after get-up time, but still the bell had not rung. She imagined the old caretaker pulling harder and harder on the rope, trying to get a sound to come out of the bell.

Finally, at 7 A.M., a whole hour later than normal, the bell clanged, and the other girls woke up. Lottie was delighted to see how confused they all were when told they were an hour late for breakfast! *I bet no one will do a better April Fools' trick than that all day,* Lottie congratulated herself.

Of course, the principal of the school was not about to let such a serious offense go unpunished. Eventually Lottie owned up to her prank. After all, she was the only girl without any blankets on her bed. Because she was so close to graduating she was not expelled, though her deportment grade was marked *D* for deficient. Lottie grimaced when she read it. She knew that her mother would not be pleased, but on the other hand, her Latin, English, and French grades were among the best in the class. Surely her mother would overlook one "little" mistake. Apparently Mrs. Moon had other concerns on her mind when she read Lottie's report card, because nothing was ever said about the failing grade in deportment.

The end of the school year finally arrived, and with it Lottie's graduation from Hollins Institute. The graduation ceremony was held in the Enon Baptist Church, which Lottie had visited as little as possible during her last year at the institute. The girls all sat in the front pews, looking nearly identical in their starched white dresses and powder blue sashes. Each graduating student had some role to play in the ceremony as a way of demonstrating that the school had turned her into a proper young lady. Some girls sang songs or played the piano or violin. Those who had written essays or poems had them read aloud by the male staff members. This was because everyone knew it was not proper for a young woman to get up and address an audience with men in it. Women never did public speaking in a mixed group. Lottie sat and fiddled as the principal read the commencement speech. The speech was all about the proper role of women in their changing world, and its main point was that no matter how smart a woman was, her role was to look after her family and be silent in church.

As she fidgeted, Lottie wondered what her sister Orie would think of such a speech. It was just the opposite of what Orie said and did. Orie believed the church held women back from having a full and interesting life, and she often wrote to Lottie telling her that she should learn to think for herself and not follow the other girls in the class.

Lottie took her advice as much as possible. A number of the girls in her class were already engaged to be married. Lottie, though, was not yet ready to be a wife, and with no father to make her marry and no money worries, she had no reason to rush into anything she did not want to do.

That was the trouble, though. Although Lottie had a long list of things she did not want to do, there was nothing on her list of things she wanted to do. As she sat in the carriage on her way back to Viewmont, she wondered what would happen next in her life. She was fifteen years old with a much better education than most other southern girls, and she had absolutely no idea what good it would do her.

Chapter 3

The Most Educated Woman in the South

At first Lottie was glad to be back at Viewmont. She had servants to lay out her clothes in the morning and bring her warm water to wash with. No bells tolled to rule her day, and she was free to sit on the lawn and read Latin or French books or take a carriage ride to visit some of her cousins on nearby plantations. But after a while, all this began to get a little boring. It was then that her mother suggested that she might like to take over the task of teaching five-year-old Edmonia. Lottie agreed and soon found that she enjoyed teaching her little sister very much. Eddie was a fast learner and especially loved acting out simple plays with Lottie.

Orie returned home for Christmas 1856. She was now a fully licensed doctor. She had achieved her goal. Orie and one other graduate were the first two female doctors in the entire South. However, even after all her hard work, Orie could not find a single hospital that would consider employing a female doctor. She came home for Christmas bitter and more committed than ever to Elizabeth Blackwell and her women's rights movement.

Surprisingly it was the Baptist church that gave Lottie an idea about what to do next with her life. The Baptists had been paying attention to the women's rights movement, and although they were not willing to say that women should be educated alongside men, they did agree that women should have access to all of the same educational opportunities as men. This was a new idea, and it created much controversy within the church. Eventually the Reverend John Broadus of the nearby Charlottesville Baptist Church organized the Albemarle Female Institute of Charlottesville. The institute was to be run on radical new lines never tried in the South. The young women enrolled in the school would take exactly the same courses, such as ancient and modern languages, natural sciences, mathematics, moral philosophy, history, and literature, as the men took at the University of Virginia.

Many people viewed this approach as scandalous and doomed to fail. They argued that the only women who could afford such an education did not need it because they had enough money to marry well and be taken care of financially for the rest of their lives. In the minds of these people, an overeducated woman with no outlet in society could be very dangerous!

Lottie was more than ready for the challenge. She enrolled at the Albemarle Female Institute in September 1857, eager to learn. The institute offered her a little more freedom than Hollins Institute had. The young women were allowed to entertain male visitors under the watchful eye of a chaperone, and the professors arranged musicals, lectures, and dances for the women to attend. The students also were encouraged to attend the Reverend Broadus's church, though Lottie made it clear from the start that she would not be going. On the first Sunday, while the other girls were gathering their Bibles for church, Lottie picked up a copy of *Twelfth Night*, a play by William Shakespeare, and announced that she was going to lie on a haystack and read the play instead of going to church.

Even though Lottie would not join the other young women in Christian activities, she soon became very popular. She was a quick learner and always had time to help the other students with their Greek or Latin translation work. She still loved to play practical jokes, and when she told the class that her middle initial *D* stood for "Devil," they all believed her.

By the end of her first year, Lottie had earned a diploma in Latin. She loved studying foreign languages and was top in her class in Greek, Italian, French, and Spanish.

Meanwhile Lottie's sister Orie had met with nothing but frustration in trying to get a job in an American hospital. In disgust she decided to leave the country that summer and travel to France and then go on through Europe to Jerusalem to visit her uncle, aunt, and cousins. Lottie was tempted to go with her, but the lure of learning kept her focused on her college career. She went back for a second year at the Albemarle Female Institute.

In December 1858, right after Lottie's eighteenth birthday, the Reverend Broadus arranged for a series of evangelistic meetings at the Baptist church. Lottie, of course, had no intention of wasting her time attending these services, and no one made her. In fact, Lottie quickly learned that most of her friends didn't want her to attend, as they were weary of the way she ridiculed their religious beliefs.

On the second day, however, Lottie wanted to have some fun. Since she hadn't been to church in a long time, she decided to show up for one of the Reverend Broadus's services and gather ammunition to torment her religious friends with. A buzz of conversation ran through the gathered crowd when Lottie entered the sanctuary. Lottie smiled brightly and took a seat near the front, ready to pick holes in the sermon the Reverend Broadus was about to deliver. Much to her surprise, by the end of the homily she had not found a single thing that didn't make sense to her. Since she had found nothing to mock, she began to wonder whether she had just wasted an hour.

Yet while Lottie tried not to give any more thought to the service, the Reverend Broadus's words kept popping into her mind. That night she could not sleep, thanks to a barking dog that kept her awake. As she lay in bed, Lottie began to think of the reasons why she was not a Christian. She decided it was mainly because of her childhood. As a young girl she had overheard so many arguments and debates about which denomination was right that she had become sick of hearing them. The arguments ended up turning her away from religion altogether. But as the night wore on, Lottie began to wonder whether turning her back on religion had been such a smart decision. Should she have given up on Christianity simply because some people argued about it? That didn't seem a very logical way to approach a decision. The more Lottie thought about it, the more she recalled the Reverend Broadus's words and the more appealing becoming a Christian seemed to her.

By the following morning, December 21, 1858, Lottie Moon had made up her mind. She wanted to become a Christian, and she didn't care who knew about it. She got up early to attend one of the special prayer meetings the students were holding in conjunction with the Reverend Broadus's meetings. As she walked in the door, Lottie watched as one girl's eyes grew wide. "We've been praying for you, but we didn't think you'd come!" the girl blurted out. "Just you watch," whispered another girl. "Lottie Moon thinks she's too clever to become a Christian; she's just here to stir up trouble."

As the meeting proceeded, however, it became clear to everyone that Lottie was not about to make trouble; she was there to learn. Rumors were soon flying around the school; was their chief skeptic a new convert? They didn't have to wait long to find out. That evening, Lottie attended another of the Reverend Broadus's meetings. This time, though, when he asked for anyone who wanted to become a Christian to come to the front, Lottie stood and marched to the altar. It was official. There was no denying it. Lottie Moon was a Christian.

Lottie asked to be baptized as soon as possible, and a baptismal service was arranged for the following evening. Before her baptism, Lottie addressed the congregation and told them why she was taking the step she was taking. In the Baptist church, this was the only time a woman was allowed to speak to a congregation that included men. Lottie assumed she would never have such an opportunity again, and so she took advantage of it.

Lottie soon became one of the most influential Christians in the Albemarle Female Institute. She ran Bible studies and prayer meetings, attended church three times a week, and helped out with Sunday school when she went home for summer breaks.

It took Lottie two more years at the institute to earn a master of arts degree. She was among the first five women to do so. The degrees were the first master's degrees ever earned by women in the South, and because Lottie graduated top of her class, she was declared the "most educated woman in the South."

Normally such an honor would have opened a door of opportunity for Lottie, perhaps as a professor at a women's college or headmistress at a preparatory school. However, on April 12, 1861, a month before she graduated, Confederate artillery in South Carolina opened fire on Fort Sumter at the entrance to Charleston harbor, which was manned by the U.S. army. The attack was the climax of a long series of disagreements between northern states and southern states over the interpretation of the U.S. Constitution. Lottie had heard these disagreements being discussed endlessly around dinner tables and on buggy rides, but she, like most other people, was shocked that the North and the South were now firing at each other.

Basically the North was in favor of the federal government's having broad rights over all of the states in the Union, while the South wanted the federal government to have very limited powers. The southern states wanted to make their own decisions and fund their own projects. The North and South had already clashed over a number of issues, including who should pay for new roads and railways in the West, taxes on manufactured goods, and one issue that did not start off being very important but quickly grew into a big issue: slavery. In the beginning, the North did not want to ban slavery in the South but rather wanted to prohibit slavery in any new western states. The South was afraid that if this ban happened, there would eventually be so many "free" states in the Union that they could, and most probably would, vote to outlaw slavery everywhere. As a result, the shots fired at Fort Sumter marked the beginning of the War Between the States, or the Civil War, as it came to be known.

At first the war did not have much impact on Lottie's life. Lottie returned to Viewmont for the summer, which turned out to be a much livelier time than the summer before, mostly because Orie had returned from her overseas jaunt. Lottie was a little nervous about telling her older sister she had become a Christian. After all, the two of them had spent hours discussing how the church was not helping the plight of women. She was in for a big surprise, though. Orie had become a Christian herself and had been baptized by her uncle James in Jerusalem! So the two sisters still had a lot in common to talk about.

Throughout the summer Orie regaled Lottie with stories of her overseas travel. "I've been waiting for so long to tell you this one," Orie told Lottie one hot afternoon as they sat together on the veranda. "I was on the foredeck of the ship all alone when a sailor came quietly up behind me and put his arm on my shoulder. 'Aren't you afraid of traveling alone?' he asked in a creepy voice."

"What did you do?" Lottie asked breathlessly. This was a terrible predicament for a southern belle to find herself in.

Orie grinned. "I knew I had to show him I was capable of taking care of myself, so I pulled out my pistol from under my skirt, aimed at the nearest seagull, and fired!"

"Oh, Orie, you didn't!" exclaimed Lottie, knowing full well her sister would do something like that.

"I surely did," said Orie, "and I hit it, too. It plummeted into the water. Then I turned and smiled at the sailor. 'Thank you for inquiring,' I said in my most charming voice, 'but I think I can look after myself if I need to, wouldn't you agree?' You should have seen his face, Lottie. It was as white as my handkerchief!"

Lottie laughed. Her sister might be a Christian now, but she hadn't lost any of her spunk.

As the summer wore on, the war began to find its way into the lives of those at Viewmont, in small ways at first. The Confederate government was desperately short of money to wage war, and the newly elected Confederate president, Jefferson Davis, called for all good southerners to bring their silver currency to banks so that it could be converted into IOUs or bonds. Lottie stayed home to watch over the plantation while Mrs. Moon and Orie made the buggy ride into Charlottesville to convert all of the family's money into Confederate bonds.

The two women arrived back at Viewmont with startling information. Confederate troops were massing near Manassas Junction to fight the Union army that had gathered by a creek named Bull Run. The war was creeping closer to home.

"I think there is going to be a lot of bloodshed, and the army will need every doctor it can get its hands on—man or woman!" Orie told Lottie. "So I signed up right away."

On July 21, 1861, news reached Viewmont that the Union and Confederate armies had clashed in the Battle of Bull Run, the first major battle of the Civil War. Confederate troops had won the day, causing the Union soldiers to retreat to Washington, D.C. Of course, there had been a lot of bloodshed, and within a day, General Cocke had sent a dispatch to Orie asking her to help set up a surgical ward in the University of Virginia buildings. It was time for every southerner to do his or her part. Ike Moon rushed off to enlist in the Confederate army, while Lottie and her sisters Colie and Mollie went along with Orie to help as nurses.

The work was more emotionally harrowing than physically hard for Lottie, who did not particularly enjoy being around dying and injured men. Since modesty did not permit the women to touch the men, the "nurses" had to content themselves with cleaning the wards, writing letters home for the soldiers, and reading aloud to help them pass the time. Lottie was thankful when Orie asked her to handle the paperwork for the ward, and she returned to Viewmont, where she set up one of the bedrooms as the hospital office.

Lottie and her mother had to attend to many other responsibilities now that Ike was off fighting. There were gardens to be supervised, crops to be planted, slaves to clothe and feed, letters to write, and socks to knit for the soldiers. Lottie also went back to supervising her little sister Eddie's schoolwork. She was busier than she'd ever been before.

Confederate President Jefferson Davis had promised that the war would be over fast and the "barbarian northerners" would once and for all be put in their place. Soon everyone could see that was an empty promise. The war was going to be a long, drawn-out affair. Battle lines were drawn all the way from Virginia to New Orleans.

With a continual flow of wounded soldiers arriving each day from the battlefield, Orie was overcome with exhaustion within a year. She had seen enough bloodshed and death to last a lifetime, and one day while sawing off a soldier's gangrene-ridden arm she collapsed. She decided she needed to take a break from the daily carnage she was witnessing. Orie returned to Viewmont, where Lottie took on the task of nursing her older sister back to health.

Not long after Orie's return, a doctor whom Orie had served alongside came to visit her. His name was Dr. John Andrews, and he came to repay a debt. When his brother died in the hospital, Dr. Andrews had lacked the money to take the body back home to Alabama for burial. Seeing his need, Orie had loaned him the money, and now he had come to repay it. He also had come to ask her to marry him. Orie was overjoyed at the prospect of marrying this fellow doctor, and their wedding ceremony took place in November.

Soon after the wedding, John Andrews was assigned to Richmond, the Confederate capital. Orie went with him. She soon discovered she was pregnant and returned to the safety of Viewmont to have the baby.

The war dragged on. Ike Moon was wounded in battle but lived to tell about it. Lottie and her sisters tried their hardest to keep the plantation going with a steadily dwindling supply of equipment and labor. Orie gave birth to a baby boy, who was quickly followed by two more babies.

The war was not going well for the Confederacy. Finally the news that everyone in the South both dreaded and expected arrived at Viewmont. On April 9, 1865, Confederate General Robert E. Lee had surrendered to Union army General Ulysses S. Grant at Appomattox Courthouse. The war that had lasted four long years was at an end.

Surrender did not bring an immediate end to Virginia's problems, however. Appomattox was only forty miles south of Viewmont, and soon victorious Union soldiers were swarming through the countryside, looting and burning homes and warehouses.

It wasn't long before word reached the women at Viewmont that Union soldiers had burned down nearby Carter's Mill. Lottie watched as her mother's face grew pale at the news. Even Orie, who was about to have another baby, looked scared. Eventually, Mrs. Moon regained her composure and took the lead. "We must act quickly," she said. "Viewmont will be next to be looted and burned."

Lottie, Orie, and their mother sprang into action.

Chapter 4

Changes

"We'll get the food and clothing," yelled Mrs. Moon, grabbing Orie's hand and heading toward the pantry. "Lottie, you get Mollie to tell Uncle Jacob to bring the wagon to the front of the house ready to load up, and then you and Colie gather the jewels and silver and bury them somewhere."

Lottie lifted her hooped skirt and ran up the stairs. She raced to find her younger sisters to give them their instructions. Once she had done this, she ran into her mother's bedroom and yanked open the top drawer of the bureau. She pulled a blue velvet bag from the drawer containing the Moon family jewels. Satisfied she had them all, Lottie grabbed two pillowcases from the linen cupboard and stuffed the jewelry into one of them. As she ran out of the bedroom, she intercepted Colie standing at the top of the stairs with her mouth wide open and her eyes blank. "Come on," Lottie said, yanking at her sister's sleeve. "We have to get the silver."

The two sisters headed downstairs to the dining room.

"Can you see any soldiers yet?" Lottie yelled as she caught a glimpse of Orie heaving a side of bacon onto the wagon.

"No," she yelled back. "But they can't be far away."

Lottie ran into the dining room. "Here, put the cutlery in this," she said, thrusting a pillowcase into Colie's hands. "I'll get the trays and the tea- and coffeepots."

"What are we going to do with them?" Colie asked as she pulled the silver forks from the sideboard drawer.

"We'll bury them in the orchard," Lottie replied, thinking up a plan as she spoke. "The ground there has just been plowed, and it will be hard for Lincoln's men to see fresh shovel marks."

"Good thinking," Colie said. "I have all the cutlery."

"Great," Lottie said, throwing the last sugar bowl into her pillowcase. "Let's go."

On the way out the door, Lottie grabbed the shovel from the fireplace. Outside, the slave, Uncle Jacob, was steadying the horse while Orie and Mrs. Moon packed clothes onto the wagon.

"Seen anything yet?" Lottie asked.

Orie stood up and shaded the sun from her eyes with her hand. "I see smoke rising from Carter's Mill," she gasped. "Hurry!"

Lottie hoisted the heavy pillowcase over her shoulder and, shovel in hand, headed for the apple orchard as fast as she could. She could hear Colie's heavy breathing a few steps behind her.

By the time they reached the apple trees, they were both out of breath. "How about burying it here?" Colie asked between gasps.

Lottie shook her head. "It's too obvious," she said. "We have to bury it somewhere where it will be hard to find."

The two sisters dragged the pillowcases down the rows of trees. "How about here?" Colie asked again.

"That looks fine," Lottie replied. "Just put a tiny mark on the tree there that only we can recognize so we can dig it up later."

Lottie ran farther down the row and found a second spot beside another tree. She began digging with her hands while she waited for Colie to finish with the fireplace shovel. After every few scoops of dirt, Lottie looked around, fully expecting to see Union soldiers coming over the rise. Soon both pillowcases of silver were buried and the dirt replaced over them so that it was impossible to tell that the ground had been disturbed.

Lottie and Colie ran back to the house to wash their hands and see what else they could do to help.

There was not much. Their mother had dispatched Uncle Jacob to hide the wagon several miles away in the thick bushes that lay on the outskirts of their property. Now all they could do was wait. Lottie tried not to think of the awful stories she had read about the Union soldiers and their raids. She knew that farther south many plantation owners had fled their land, only to return to find all of the buildings burned to the ground, their livestock killed and eaten, and their slaves scattered. Lottie hoped her family would fare better than that, but she knew that whatever happened, now that the war was ending, their lives would be very different from before.

Like most people in the South, Lottie had no idea what peace with the North would mean. She wondered how people in the South could go back to being part of one country after the Union army had killed so many young southern men, not to mention the destruction Sherman's men had caused as they rampaged through Georgia. Lottie sighed; so much hatred and bitterness flowed between the two sides. She had little doubt in her mind that she would never again enjoy the innocent life she had lived before the war. Even if the North managed to show some kindness to the South, the plantation way of life her ancestors had practiced was no longer possible. President Abraham Lincoln had issued a proclamation freeing all slaves, and most of the railroads and many of the grand old plantations in the South had been destroyed. Besides, there seemed to be no point in going back to producing cotton, even if they could find the workers. Great Britain, which had purchased most of the South's cotton, had found a new supply from India.

Lottie and her mother and sisters waited into the night, but no Union soldiers came. They all slept fitfully in the parlor with the door barred and Orie's trusty pistol close at hand. The following morning they learned that the cloud of smoke they had seen rising from Carter's Mill was not the plantation burning but the dust kicked up by a herd of sheep being driven to Scottsville. Everyone was relieved, yet the possibility of Union fighters ransacking Viewmont was a continual threat for several more weeks until the last few bands of Confederate soldiers surrendered and the Civil War was officially declared over.

Lottie watched as many of the family slaves wrapped their few meager belongings in knapsacks and set out for the North to find their own way in life. A number, however, chose to stay on the Viewmont property, though there was little for them to do. Mrs. Moon, like most other plantation owners, faced some serious choices. There simply was not enough money to pay former slaves to work. The Confederate bonds she had converted the family's currency into at the beginning of the war were not even worth the paper they were printed on. To make matters worse, the two bags of silver and jewelry that Lottie and Colie had buried in the orchard could not be found. Had someone else dug them up, or in the panic of the moment had the two girls become confused about exactly where they buried the bags? No one knew. In fact, the bags would never be found.

The end of the war also left the other members of the Moon family with some tough decisions to make. Orie and her husband, John Andrews, decided to go to Alabama with their three sons. They wanted to help John's father rebuild his farm. Meanwhile, Ike Moon, who was now married, asked his mother to give him four hundred acres of Viewmont land for a farm of his own. He soon found, however, that he could not manage the farm on his own, and he sold the piece of land. It was the first of many parcels of Viewmont land to leave the family's hands.

Whatever happened, Lottie's mother was determined to give Eddie and Mollie a good education. She leased out the rest of Viewmont's land, except for the house, orchard, and cemetery, in exchange for one third of the proceeds from the crops raised on it. She used this money to keep herself and Colie and to send Eddie and Mollie to the Richmond Female Institute. This took all the money she had. The two younger girls were not able to come home for the holidays because Mrs. Moon could not afford their coach fares.

In the midst of all the changes the war had brought, Lottie had her own decisions to make. Before the war she had toyed with the idea of having a career, simply for the satisfaction of having it. Now that the war was over, however, getting a job and earning her own money became an urgent matter.

As Lottie pondered what to do next, the Reverend Broadus received a letter from the First Baptist Church in Danville, Kentucky, asking whether he could recommend a woman to assist at the female academy the church was running. The Reverend Broadus visited Lottie and explained that her name was the first that had come to mind when he read the letter. Lottie was excited by the prospect. It was just the opportunity she had been looking for, and within a week she was packed and ready to go.

Danville, like just about every other city in the South, was in a state of turmoil, with hundreds of war widows and orphaned or abandoned children roaming throughout the area. The principal of the female academy there, the Reverend Selph, a kind-hearted man, had given away many scholarships to the daughters of destitute Baptist pastors. Because of his generosity, the school was never quite able to cover all of its costs. Nevertheless, Lottie came to feel very much at home there. After her first year, she signed up for a second and recruited her sister Mollie to join her as a junior staff member.

Besides teaching a variety of subjects, Lottie busied herself teaching a Sunday school class for teenage girls. It was lively and fun, and all the young girls in the church counted down the months until they were old enough to join the group. Lottie also spent time visiting Dr. George Burton, who had been a Southern Baptist medical missionary in China. Dr. Burton had returned to the United States just before the Civil War broke out and had been unable to return because of the conflict and a lack of money. As a result, he had turned his attention to raising money to help support his fellow missionaries in China and, whenever he had the opportunity, to speaking to church groups about the needs of China.

Lottie listened to all Dr. Burton had to say. The idea of being a missionary piqued her interest, though there were two things that made it only a dream. First, Lottie was a single woman, and the only women the Southern Baptists would send overseas were married. Second, since the end of the Civil War, not one missionary had been sent out by the church. The Southern Baptists were too poor to pay the salary for a new missionary. Indeed, to save money, they had recalled a number of missionaries from the mission field.

Lottie kept in touch with her family by letter, though many of the letters she received back from her mother were upsetting. Mrs. Moon seemed to be in a state of constant despair, and she usually asked Lottie for more money to help pay the taxes on the property. Colie had left home to teach in Bristol, Virginia, and she too sent money to try to keep Viewmont in the hands of the Moon family.

Besides the possibility of losing Viewmont, another issue upset Mrs. Moon very much. Lottie's two younger sisters, Mollie and Colie, had done the unthinkable; both had decided to convert to Roman Catholicism. Colie was even talking about entering a convent and becoming a nun. Their decision shocked Mrs. Moon. The girls' father had built the biggest Baptist church for miles around, and she had raised her daughters to follow in the family tradition of being Baptist. She poured out her anguish over their decision in letter after letter to Lottie, who wrote back urging her mother to be loving and tolerant of their decision. However, their conversion to Catholicism was one shock too many for Mrs. Moon. She decided life was no longer worth living. She lay in bed refusing to eat or drink anything and just stared blankly at the wall. Lottie hurried home to her bedside, but she could do nothing to change her mother's mind and persuade her to eat. Anna Maria Moon, Lottie's mother, died on June 21, 1870, at sixty-one years of age.

Mrs. Moon's will was read, and the land was distributed according to her wishes, although there was little money left to distribute. The estate was worth only a fortieth of what it had been worth before the Civil War. Lottie received a small allowance, but since it was not enough to live on, she would have to keep working or get married.

That fall, Lottie returned to Danville for her fourth year of teaching. By now she was the head teacher of history, grammar, and literature. When she arrived back at school, a new teacher by the name of Anna Safford was waiting to meet her.

Much to Lottie's relief, Anna's strong teaching subjects were mathematics and astronomy, the two subjects Lottie most disliked teaching.

Lottie and Anna soon discovered that in many ways they had led very similar lives. Anna was three years older than Lottie, single, intelligent, lively, kind, and a strong Christian. Both women had been forced to work after their families had lost their fortunes as a result of the Civil War.

There were some differences between the two as well. Anna was as firm a Presbyterian as Lottie was a Baptist. After a few disagreements, the two of them decided not to discuss their differing ideas about baptism and a few other doctrinal issues and instead stick to discussing topics they could agree on. A strong friendship quickly developed between the two women, and soon Lottie and Anna found they had another thing in common: Both harbored a secret dream of becoming a missionary, though neither of them came from a church that was willing to send out single women as missionaries.

Although Lottie and Anna could see no obvious way to make their dream a reality, they often discussed ways they could both be more useful. They wondered whether they should head farther south, where the need for teachers to educate girls was critical. The Civil War had changed southern society, and many girls who would have looked forward to marriage and a comfortable home supplied by their husbands now had to find ways to support themselves. Over 135,000 southern men had been killed in the war, and there were now simply not enough men to meet the demand for husbands. Plus, many of the men who survived the war had been left wounded or had lost all or most of their land and money.

In March 1871, Lottie received a letter from her cousin Pleasant Moon. Pleasant had moved out of Virginia and had become a successful merchant in Cartersville, Georgia. In his letter he told Lottie that he and several other businessmen in town had set up a board of trustees for a girls school. They had many students waiting to attend, and they had even picked a building to hold the school in. All they needed now were teachers.

Lottie's heart raced as she read the letter. Could this be the challenge she had been waiting for? She hurried off to tell Anna about it.

Chapter 5

Surely They'll Send You

As the train chugged slowly southward, Lottie Moon and Anna Safford peered out the window of their carriage at the changing scenery. It was lush and green, as the South always was at this time of year. But the countryside was also dotted with the still visible signs of the ravages of the Civil War. Brick and stone chimneys, all that remained of once glorious plantation homes, stood as gaunt monuments to a southern way of life the war had destroyed. At the sight of such chimneys, Lottie often found her mind drifting back to Viewmont and the very different life she had once lived there.

Finally the train pulled into Cartersville, Georgia, and waiting at the station was Pleasant Moon. "Hello, ladies," he bellowed as the train hissed to a halt.

Lottie leaned out the window and waved. "Pleasant, how pleasant to see you!" she teased, using the greeting she and her cousins had always used when they saw him.

Pleasant laughed. "You haven't changed one bit for all your schooling, Lottie!" He took off his hat and bowed slightly. "Miss Safford, I presume?" he said.

Anna smiled. "Yes, indeed. It is good to meet you at last, Mr. Moon."

Pleasant turned to the helper he had brought along with him. "You wait here while the ladies get off the train, and I'll see to their luggage," he said.

By the time Lottie and Anna had climbed down from the train, Pleasant had claimed their trunks. While his helper loaded the trunks onto the wagon, Pleasant helped the two women climb aboard and get seated on one of the wagon's hard wooden seats.

"How are you, Lottie? You must be exhausted," Pleasant inquired as he guided the wagon away from the station.

"Not nearly as tired as I would be if I had come by stagecoach. Trains are a much smoother and more comfortable way to travel," she replied. "Anna and I have been waiting forever to hear about our new school. Tell us all about it."

Pleasant cleared his throat and looked down. Lottie's heart skipped a beat. "Is something wrong?" she asked.

"Well, not exactly," replied her cousin. "We do have a schoolhouse, of sorts, and some students..." His voice trailed off.

"Then tell us about the schoolhouse," Lottie said eagerly.

"Well, buildings are hard to come by, as I am sure you can appreciate. The Union army burned virtually every structure it could to the ground. However, we were able to find an old cannery. It has three rooms, one large and two smaller, and the canning stoves have been stripped out of the building."

Pleasant looked up at Lottie apologetically. In an instant she knew why he was embarrassed. The last time the two had met, Lottie had been the pampered daughter of a very wealthy family, able to have the best of everything life could offer. And now, here was Lottie's cousin offering her a low-paying job as a teacher in a school that would be run in an old cannery!

Lottie smiled bravely. "Time has certainly changed our circumstances, Pleasant," she assured her cousin. "Anna and I will be happy to do whatever we can to teach the girls of Cartersville, in an old cannery or anywhere else."

A look of relief crept across Pleasant's face. Then, gingerly, Pleasant proceeded. "We've sent out flyers and talked to hundreds of people, but we have only seven girls enrolled so far."

"That's a start," Lottie said, trying to sound a lot more hopeful than she felt.

Soon the wagon pulled up in front of Pleasant's home, where the two women were to stay for as long as they wanted.

When Lottie finally got to see the cannery classroom, her heart sank. It had no equipment, not even a desk in the place, and weeds grew high around the edges of the building's brick walls. A number of the windows were broken as well.

After a few moments, Lottie regained her composure and brightly announced to Anna, "Well, we had better get to work! The first thing we need to do is make a list of everything we need."

Soon the two young women were hard at work transforming the old cannery into a school. Since no funds were available to purchase the supplies they needed, they spent their own money buying books and science equipment, along with a piano and an organ. After they had pulled the weeds from the overgrown shrubbery around the buildings, they planted trees and flowers in their place.

It took only a few days after the start of the school year for news to spread. By the end of the first week, enrollment was up to thirty, and within two months, one hundred girls were attending class. This kept the two teachers of the Cartersville School for Young Ladies busy, but not busy enough for Lottie. The more she had to do, the more energy she seemed to have. Once again, she volunteered to teach Sunday school. She also often accompanied the Reverend Headden, the local Baptist pastor, on his visits to some of the most desperate people in town.

The year passed quickly, and all of Cartersville seemed happy with the new school. Indeed, enrollment was even higher for the start of the second year, and Lottie and Anna looked forward to getting back to teaching classes again.

Something happened during that year that both shocked and unsettled Lottie. It had to do with the letter she received from her youngest sister, Edmonia. The letter was dated April 16, 1872, and Lottie had to read it three times before its full impact hit. Somehow Eddie had managed to get herself appointed as a single female missionary to China. What was more astonishing was that by the time Lottie received the letter, Edmonia was already well on her way there!

After getting over the initial shock of the letter, Lottie began to piece together the extraordinary events that led to her younger sister's being sent as a single woman missionary to China. Eddie had been missionary secretary at the Richmond Female Institute, and one of her duties while in that position was to write to Tarleton and Martha Crawford, who had gone out as missionaries to China in 1851. Eddie and Lottie had often discussed what was happening in Tengchow, China, where the Crawfords now lived. In fact, the two sisters had committed to send forty-five dollars in gold to support the school Martha Crawford had opened there. (This had been a large sum of money for them to raise on their incomes.)

According to Edmonia's letter, the Southern Baptist Foreign Mission Board had given permission for another single woman, Lula Whilden of South Carolina, to accompany her sister and brother-in-law to Canton, China, to help in missionary work among the women there. The board had approved this because Lula would not be working alone but would be living in the same house as her married sister. As a result, Eddie decided that since the Foreign Mission Board had allowed one single woman to go to China as a missionary, it should allow any single women who wanted to go there the same privilege. So she wrote to Martha Crawford and asked for a letter inviting her to work with them in Tengchow. Martha obligingly wrote the letter of invitation, and Eddie began assailing the Foreign Mission Board with requests to be allowed to go and help the Crawfords in China. Finally the board agreed and gave her permission to go, as long as she paid her own way there and supplied her own living expenses, at least until some better support arrangement could be worked out for her.

Twenty-one-year-old Edmonia had jumped at the chance, and as her letter calculated, by the time Lottie read it, she would already be somewhere in the middle of the Pacific Ocean en route to China.

Lottie read the letter to Anna Safford, who was as astonished by its contents as Lottie had been.

"It hardly seems possible!" exclaimed Anna. "The Baptists are sending out a twenty-one-year-old single woman. Why, Lottie, if they'll send Edmonia, surely they'll send you!"

Lottie was having the same thought. As the year progressed, she wrote to the Reverend Henry Tupper, the secretary of the Southern Baptist Foreign

Mission Board, and asked if it might be possible for her to join her younger sister in China as a missionary. She also wrote to Edmonia to find out whether there was enough work to keep them both busy. Eddie wrote right back telling Lottie that Tarleton Crawford thought she would be perfectly suited to help in the school. At the end of the letter she added, "I cannot convince myself that it is the will of God that you shall not come. True, you are doing a noble work at home, but are there not some who could fill your place? I don't know of anyone who could fill the place offered you here. In the first place, it is not everyone who is willing to come to China. In the next place, their having the proper qualifications is doubtful."

Around this time, the Reverend Headden attended a regional Baptist pastors meeting and returned to Cartersville fired up to recruit members of his congregation to go out as foreign missionaries. On his return, he preached a rousing sermon about the need for missionaries. When he was done, Lottie slipped out of her front-row pew and hurried home. She did not eat lunch or dinner that day and instead spent the time praying about her future. When she finally emerged from her room, she was sure of one thing: God had called her to be a missionary in China. She quickly found her friend Anna to tell her the news. Much to Lottie's surprise, Anna herself had felt the same call. As a result, the Presbyterian church was preparing to send her out as a missionary to China.

June 2, 1873, was one of the most difficult days in Lottie's life. It was the day she and Anna told the students at the Cartersville School for Young Ladies that they were resigning as teachers and going to China as missionaries. Many of the girls sobbed quietly after the announcement was made.

Some of the girls' parents had a different reaction. They asked Pleasant Moon and the school's board why two talented young women would want to waste themselves on the heathen in some far-off country. Didn't they know there were good southern girls who needed an education?

Still, as time passed, people began to adjust to the fact that the two women would be leaving, and another teacher was hired to take their place. With the arrival of the new teacher, it was time for Lottie to concentrate on getting to China.

The women of the First Baptist Church in Cartersville were excited to think that someone they knew, a woman no less, was going to China as a missionary. It all sounded so adventurous and bold to them. They banded together and formed a women's missionary society to help Lottie with money and moral support.

Lottie purchased a ticket to China aboard the *Costa Rica,* a three-masted square-rigged sailing ship. The vessel was due to sail from San Francisco on September 1, 1873. Lottie estimated it would take her two weeks to travel by train on the new transcontinental railway to get to San Francisco, leaving her a month to visit her sister Orie and her growing family.

Orie and her husband, John Andrews, lived in Lauderdale County, on the Alabama-Tennessee state line. By now Orie had given birth to six sons, though three of them already had died from childhood illnesses. The two sisters had a wonderful reunion, and Orie taught Lottie as much as she could about the effects of various medicines and how to care for the sick. In the evenings, Lottie wrote long letters to her many friends, explaining to them why she was going to China. She also wrote an open letter to Southern Baptist churches. It took her a long time to find the right words, but eventually she wrote and encouraged the young men of the church to take up their place in missions. At the end of the letter she added: "For women, too, foreign missions open a new and enlarged sphere of labor and furnish opportunities for good which angels might almost envy.... Could a Christian woman possibly desire higher honor than to be permitted to go from house to house and tell of a Savior to those who have never heard His name? We could not conceive a life which would more thoroughly satisfy the mind and heart of a true follower of the Lord Jesus."

The letter sounded wonderfully challenging, though Lottie herself had no real idea of the struggles and challenges that lay ahead of her on the other side of the world.

It was a sad moment when Lottie finally had to say good-bye to Orie. She knew she would probably never see her older sister or her nephews again.

After all, she had signed the standard Baptist missionary contract stating that she was committed to staying in China until a "total breakdown of health, or death."

Lottie consoled herself with the thought that she would be joining Edmonia in China. In that respect, Lottie knew that she was more fortunate than most other missionaries headed for China; none of them had a blood relative eagerly awaiting their arrival. Yet it was still difficult to leave behind in America Orie and her family, her younger sisters Mollie, who had married Dr. William Shepherd and now lived in Norfolk, Virginia, and Colie, who was working at the Treasury Department in Washington, D.C., and her older brother Isaac and his wife, who were back trying to eke out a living at Viewmont.

The train to San Francisco raced along at twenty-two miles per hour, transporting Lottie in two weeks from one side of the American continent to the other. The transcontinental railroad had been completed less than five years before, and it was still a great novelty for those riding on the train to see the old established cities of the East give way to the huge rolling prairies, and then to the towering, majestic Rocky Mountains. Lottie spent hours looking out the window. She had never seen such breathtaking scenery. She felt almost as if she were in a foreign country already. Finally the train crossed the last of the mountain ranges and began puffing its way down the last leg of the journey to

San Francisco and the Pacific Ocean. On the other side of this sparkling ocean that Lottie was finally seeing for the first time lay China.

Chapter 6

China at Last

The *Costa Rica* lay at anchor in the calm waters of San Francisco Bay. Two days after arriving in San Francisco by train, Lottie was ferried out to the ship. She clambered aboard, eager to be on her way to her new life as a missionary. Lottie was the only single woman on the voyage, and she soon made friends with almost everyone aboard, including six couples from various denominations who were on their way to Japan and China to be missionaries.

Once the last-minute details were taken care of and they set sail, there was little for the passengers to do. The sea was unusually calm, and they passed the time playing cards and chess, listening to lectures, and reading. Despite the calm, Lottie was glad when the coastline around Yokohama, Japan, finally came into view on September 21. It was her first sea voyage, and she had not been able to adjust to the constant rocking motion of the ship.

Yokohama was the first of three ports in Japan where the *Costa Rica* was scheduled to stop. From Yokohama they sailed on to Kobe and Nagasaki. At each port, Lottie eagerly disembarked and hired a rickshaw driver to show her the sights of the city. She was enchanted by everything she saw, especially the gardens. Lottie had never seen such beautifully kept lawns or artistically designed rock-and-water gardens. She tried to recall every detail so that she could accurately describe the places in letters back home to her family.

On September 28, 1873, the *Costa Rica* set sail from Nagasaki for Shanghai, China. The voyage should have taken only several days, except for the hurricane! The vicious storm struck without warning the first night out from Nagasaki. Lottie was already in bed in her topside cabin with the lamp turned out when the ship began to creak and roll ominously from side to side. Soon she could hear heavy objects crashing against the side of her cabin, bashing first against one wall and then against the other. Lottie stayed in her bunk and prayed feverishly, but the sound of shattering glass and splintering wood kept distracting her. She began to wonder whether she would make it to China after all. The storm raged on throughout the night, and by the next morning it was fiercer than ever. With the arrival of daylight, Lottie threw a coat on over her nightgown and stepped outside her cabin to see what was happening. She steadied herself against the fierce wind and hand over hand slowly made her way along the ship's mangled railing to the dining room. The dining room was a complete mess, plates and glasses lay shattered on the floor, and the windows, along with one entire wall, were gone.

"Over here," yelled Mr. Whitehead, one of the missionaries, over the howl of the wind.

Lottie staggered over to the corner where several of the missionary couples were seated on the floor. "What's happening?" she asked.

"Most of the crew are out on deck trying to keep the mast from breaking," Mr. Whitehead replied. "And the ship's surgeon and most of the other passengers are down below drinking whiskey. Some of them are so drunk they would probably fall overboard even if the ship was sailing on a millpond!"

"I'm glad I found you," Lottie replied. "I'm sure God will have His way with this ship one way or the other."

The group prayed and sang together throughout the rest of the morning. Finally around midday the force of the hurricane began to subside, although the crisis was not yet over. The *Costa Rica* had sustained heavy damage, its rudder had been swept away, the main mast was broken, and large portions of the upper deck had been washed overboard. There was no way to steer the ship, which drifted aimlessly.

Finally the captain and crew were able to regain some control over their ship, and the *Costa Rica* limped back to Nagasaki. Everyone aboard was glad to see land. As soon as they dropped anchor, they made plans to repair the ship. By now Lottie was so exhausted that it was two days before she had the strength to disembark ship and take advantage of the hospitality of some Dutch Reformed Church missionaries. She stayed with them a week until the *Costa Rica* was repaired and ready to set sail again.

This time the voyage to Shanghai was as smooth as the trip across the Pacific Ocean from San Francisco had been. On October 7, 1873, Charlotte (Lottie) Digges Moon finally set foot in China. Tarleton and Martha Crawford, along with the Reverend Matthew Yates, were waiting to meet her and escort her to the Reverend Yates's home, where they would all be staying for several days.

Lottie was a little surprised that Edmonia hadn't come to meet her. Tarleton Crawford explained that someone had to stay behind to supervise the building of the wonderful two-story extension he was having added onto his house. This four-room tower was being built for Edmonia and Lottie to share. Of course, Lottie was impressed, but she was also impatient to see her sister. To her dismay, she would have to wait in Shanghai for a week while Tarleton Crawford conducted some private business. Martha Crawford explained that during the Civil War very little support money had been sent to the missionaries in China. Rather than go home, Tarleton had gone into business for himself, buying and selling land in China at a profit, and his dealings in Shanghai were related to this business.

While they waited, Martha showed Lottie around Shanghai. They visited the international compounds where most of the foreigners in the city lived. As they wound their way through the streets of the bustling old city, Lottie was impressed by many of the sights she saw. She was appalled, however, to see the girls and women teetering along with their feet bound in half with rags in accordance with the Chinese practice of foot binding. Even though Lottie had grown up in the country, nothing could have prepared her for the sights and sounds of the Chinese market. Before she even reached it, she could smell it. She could make out the odor of fish baking in the midday sun and the putrid odor of chicken that had been dead several days too long before being sold. But there were many odors she couldn't make out, and not all the odors were bad. Her nostrils picked up the sweet smell of jasmine and orange blossom.

When she finally entered the market, Lottie was overwhelmed by what she saw. Everywhere people were buying and selling almost everything imaginable. One vendor had Chinese shoes arranged on the ground in front of him, while the next vendor sold trousers and tunics, and the next dried fish, and the next fruits and vegetables, many of which Lottie had never seen. Lottie followed Martha around the market, her mouth agape at all she was seeing.

Throughout the week, Lottie peppered Martha with questions about what it was like to live in Tengchow, where they would soon be headed. She quickly found out that there were many differences between the two cities.

"Shanghai is a treaty port, as you know," Martha explained, "and many Western ideas are tolerated here. One clause of the treaty says that any foreigner or Chinese person can practice Christianity here freely, but once you get outside the treaty ports, it's not the case. Things are more difficult."

"What kind of difficulties do you have?" asked Lottie, fearing that Eddie had cast the work in Tengchow in too bright a light.

"Well..." Martha replied slowly. "It's not easy work, I'll give you that. We are often spat upon and called foreign devils." She looked at Lottie and went on briskly. "It's more a bluff than anything, but sometimes it does get out of hand. Last month, for example, your sister and I had to stop our daily visits to some women who had invited us to their homes. A crowd of jeering men followed us everywhere we went, brandishing clubs and knives. After they chased us, yelling that they would chop off our heads, we decided it was not safe to go out for a while."

"Oh..." was all Lottie could think to say. "And how is Edmonia when it comes to ordeals like that?" she finally asked.

"Edmonia is doing fine," Martha replied, then darkly added, "for the most part." With that she would not say another word.

Lottie would have liked to have asked Martha what she meant, but it was obvious that she would have to wait to get to Tengchow to find out for herself.

Tarleton Crawford's business was taking longer than anticipated, making him rather grumpy. So Martha and Lottie decided to go on ahead to Tengchow without him. Once again, Lottie climbed aboard a boat. This time the vessel took them northward along the coast to Chefoo on the Shantung peninsula. There the two women stayed with a missionary couple, the Hartwells, while Martha hired *shentzes* that would take them overland to Tengchow. It seemed odd to Lottie that they would have to travel overland to Tengchow when it was a coastal port. Martha explained that Tengchow's harbor was quite silted up, and deep-hulled ships were unable to navigate their way into it.

The shentze reminded Lottie of a wheel-less covered wagon supported by two long poles, one on either side, attached to the saddles of two donkeys, one in the front and one at the rear. At first Lottie thought the shentze looked like a comfortable place to ride, but before they had gone half a mile down the road, she had changed her mind about that. As the shentze jolted and lurched its way sixty miles northwestward to Tengchow, it felt to Lottie as though every bone in her body was broken and bruised.

Finally, after two of the longest days in Lottie's life, the magnificent walled city of Tengchow came into view. Lottie had never seen anything quite like it. The city and its huge gray mud brick wall were over two thousand years old. What fascinated Lottie was the way the wall was designed to provide safe harbor for sampans and other small boats. The wall ran along the edge of the harbor and had openings where canals ran inside it. Large wooden gates that opened and closed to let boats in and out spanned the openings in the wall. Eighty thousand people lived in and around the old walled city.

"See there, it's the spire of the church," yelled Martha from her shentze, pointing to a high structure with a cross on top that, along with a beautifully carved Chinese gate, dominated the skyline of the city. "It cost three thousand dollars of Tarleton's own money to build, but it's worth it. Isn't it magnificent?"

"Yes," Lottie replied, eyeing the structure. "It certainly stands out."

Soon her shentze was outside the walled mission compound. Rising above the wall Lottie could see the two-story tower that Tarleton was having built for her and Edmonia.

Martha spoke to the gatekeeper in Chinese, and the gates were quickly opened. Lottie's wobbly legs hardly allowed her to stand straight as she stood in the courtyard of her new home. Edmonia appeared at the door. She looked much the same as always, perhaps a little thinner, and Lottie rushed across the courtyard to embrace her.

The two sisters had a lot to talk about. Eddie wanted to know all about her brother and sisters back in the United States, and Lottie wanted to hear all about Eddie's experiences in Tengchow. As they drank tea and talked, Lottie noticed her sister coughed a lot. "Are you all right?" she finally asked.

Edmonia smiled weakly. "Well, it hasn't been easy here, to say the least," she replied. "Some things are a terrible strain."

"What things?" Lottie asked.

Eddie looked around to make sure no one was listening and then lowered her voice and spoke. "Like the new tower Tarleton Crawford is building for us. It's caused so much trouble."

"Trouble?" repeated Lottie, feeling alarmed. "Why would it cause trouble?"

"It's the whole idea of a tower," confided her sister. "The Chinese all like to live in compounds or houses with walls around them. I suppose it's the only way they can get any privacy with so many people around."

"I've noticed that," agreed Lottie. "So what's the problem with the tower?"

"It's privacy," Eddie said. "Apparently the Chinese don't build tall buildings because someone could look out of them and down on other people inside their courtyards. When Tarleton Crawford started to build this monstrosity, there was a riot. The local men thought he was going to spy on their wives, and they stormed the gate with sticks and stones."

"What happened?" Lottie asked.

"Tarleton Crawford got out his gun and aimed it at a few of them. They fled, but I'm not sure it's all over yet. They seemed very angry."

Lottie sat in silence. She wondered how a missionary who had been in China for over twenty years could make a decision that would cause anger and suspicion among so many local people.

"And another thing," Edmonia went on. "People in America might think it's proper for single women like you and me to live with a married couple, but do you know how the Chinese view it?"

"No," Lottie said slowly, dreading what Eddie would say next.

Eddie's voice dropped even lower till it was just above a whisper. She looked into her older sister's eyes. "They think I am Tarleton Crawford's second wife, and I'm sure they will think you are his third."

Lottie felt herself blushing. "That's terrible," she replied. "What can we do about it?"

"I'm not sure," Edmonia replied. "But we will have to think of something if we expect the Chinese women to take us seriously."

Lottie and Eddie talked on, though Lottie's mind was racing with the new information she had been given. What should she do? Was Eddie right in suggesting that Tarleton Crawford was out of step with what Chinese people thought? And what about having to use the power of a gun to keep a mission house open. That didn't seem right at all. She might be a novice missionary, but Lottie decided there and then that she would never raise a gun against a Chinese person. After all, she had come to bring them the hope of a new life in Christ, and she could not see how a gun helped in any way to further that end.

Chapter 7

A Picnic in the Countryside

The day after Lottie's arrival in Tengchow, Martha Crawford took her and Edmonia to visit Sallie Holmes. Sallie was about five years older than Lottie, with an oval face and kind blue eyes. Lottie immediately liked her, and she admired her even more after hearing the story of why she lived in China.

Sallie had come to China with her husband in the mid-1850s before the treaty ports had been opened up to Westerners. The Holmeses were the first Western missionaries in Chefoo. Life there was not easy for them at first. They were often spat at and threatened, but they persevered and started a small church. Sallie gave birth to a baby girl, but the child died soon afterward. Sallie was expecting her second child when one night, about two years after moving into the area, her husband, James Landrum Holmes, was asked to ride out and talk with a band of robbers who were threatening the town. It was the last time Sallie saw her husband alive. James Holmes was brutally murdered by the band of robbers.

The murder left Sallie in a very difficult position; should she go back to the United States or stay at her mission post without a husband and with a baby on the way? She chose to stay, and since she had her own private source of income, the Foreign Mission Board was happy for her to do so. Three months after her husband's murder, Sallie gave birth to a son, whom she named Landrum. In 1862 she moved from nearby Chefoo to Tengchow.

After telling Lottie her story, Sallie changed the direction of the conversation. "Your sister has done so well learning Mandarin. She was able to take over the boys grade school within a year. Have you visited it yet?"

"No, I haven't," Lottie replied. "I have so much to see and learn in Tengchow. Mrs. Crawford is busy with her medical clinic, and she thought that perhaps you would be the best person to acquaint me with ways to reach Chinese women with the gospel."

Lottie watched Sallie's eyes light up. "I would be delighted," Sallie exclaimed. "I've been praying for a helper for so long."

The women talked on for another half hour. By the end of the conversation, it had been decided that Eddie's language teacher should be employed to help Lottie learn Mandarin, and then Lottie should help her sister with the boys school. And as soon as Lottie knew a little of the language, Sallie promised to take her out into the country on one of the fifty or so preaching trips she made each year.

Lottie spent the rest of the day checking out the boys school while Eddie spent her time planning lessons and testing the boys on their work. Lottie had been in many schools before, but watching Eddie at work in this school was very different. When the students recited their lessons for Eddie, they would turn away and face the wall. Eddie told Lottie that it was seen as disrespectful for a student to look at a teacher while he was talking to her.

The following day Lottie had her first appointment with her new Mandarin language teacher. Since she already spoke several languages fluently, Lottie did not anticipate much difficulty learning Mandarin. To her surprise, it turned out to be a lot more difficult than she had thought it would be. All of the other languages Lottie knew were based on Latin, whereas Mandarin was a tonal language. This meant that if the same sounds were made at a higher or lower pitch, they would mean two completely different things. To make matters worse, many different dialects were spoken within twenty miles of Tengchow, and if Lottie wanted to work among the women in the countryside, she would have to learn them all. This challenge gave her a new appreciation for what her sister had managed to accomplish in eleven short months.

On Sunday, Lottie was eager to go to church. She had read so many letters from Edmonia that she felt as if she already knew many of the Chinese Christians. The church itself was similar on the outside to many she had seen in the United States. It was made of gray stone blocks, and it had large double wooden front doors and a high spire. Inside, it was very different. The sanctuary was divided down the middle by a thin wooden wall. The men entered the building through the double doors at the front and sat on pews facing the pastor. The few women who attended services entered the church through a side door and sat on the other side of the wall from the men. They could not hear the sermon very clearly, and Martha Crawford spent most of her time during the service telling the women what her husband was preaching about.

When Lottie commented on the fact that there were about forty men on one side and only ten women on the other, Sallie whispered, "We have to be grateful there are any women at all in church. It's not an easy thing for them to come."

"Why not?" Lottie asked.

"Chinese women are very restricted," Sallie went on. "No doubt you have noticed there are not many of them in the markets or even walking along the streets. That's because women stay inside their compounds. It's their tradition. Only a very poor woman would venture out to run her own errands."

Lottie sat and thought about what she had been told. She had thought it was difficult being an independent woman in pre–Civil War Virginia, but the lot of women in China seemed much more restrictive. She looked down at the feet of the woman next to her and shuddered. The woman's feet were no more than four inches long, wrapped in layers of white cotton fabric. The whole idea behind foot binding horrified Lottie. Every young girl's toes were bent and tied under their feet until the bones in the foot broke and the toes turned back toward the ankles easily. The pain was so great that the girls could not walk for months at a time, and when they did manage to move around again, they hobbled slowly, never able to run or skip again. As she looked at the woman's feet, Lottie hoped that one day she could find a way to help stop the horrible practice of foot binding.

Lottie had been in Tengchow for three weeks when Martha Crawford announced it was time for her to experience life outside the city walls. "Today is Saturday, and I've arranged a picnic for us," she told the two sisters at breakfast. "Sallie Holmes is coming along, too. We will travel by sedan chair to several of the outer villages. Mr. Woo, a deacon from the church, will accompany us. Either he or I will do the preaching. We will take a picnic lunch with us and return before nightfall. It can get a little chilly, so bring a shawl."

An hour later, Lottie looked out of her second-story window to see a procession of coolies (Chinese laborers) carrying sedan chairs and making their way along the street to the mission compound.

"Come on, Eddie, it's time to go," she said, putting her language notebook into a bag and opening the door.

Edmonia followed her sister downstairs, and soon they were being helped into their sedan chairs.

"Good morning, Lottie," came a voice.

Lottie turned to see Sallie Holmes sitting on a donkey.

"A lovely day for an outing, isn't it?" Sallie said.

Lottie nodded, grabbing for the bamboo rods that supported the chair. "Do you prefer riding a donkey?" she asked.

"Most of the time," the veteran missionary replied. "They're bony creatures, but I can anticipate the jolts a little better than in a sedan chair."

Lottie nodded, making a mental note that she should learn to ride a donkey herself.

Soon the procession of coolies, sedan chairs, and missionaries set off down the road toward the town gate. Sallie led the way on her donkey, followed by Eddie in her sedan chair, and then Martha Crawford, while Lottie brought up the rear. Each sedan chair was carried by four coolies. Mr. Woo walked alongside the women. On the way to the town gate they had to pass through the local marketplace, which meant some tight maneuvering for the coolies carrying the chairs as they made their way around huge baskets of fruit and avoided mules laden with baskets of rice and millet. From her perch on the sedan chair, Lottie watched all the commotion of the marketplace. The way people cajoled and bargained with each other until they agreed on a fair price was unlike anything she had seen back in the United States. In a strange way, the people seemed to enjoy the bargaining process more than actually getting the product they wanted.

Before long they had passed through the gate and were making their way along a flat dirt track with maize fields on either side. The fields stretched back from the edge of the Yellow Sea and went on for as far as Lottie could see. There were no houses, though, to break the horizon since, as Sallie explained, Chinese farmers lived in walled villages and walked out to their land and back each day. They did this because they did not want to spend the night outside the wall where they could fall prey to bands of robbers.

Soon Sallie trotted up on her donkey beside Lottie. "Martha has decided we should head northwest," she said. "We are going to a village we have never been to before. We'll probably be the first white people many of the Chinese there have ever seen. That should draw us a good crowd," she added with a laugh.

Lottie laughed, too, though a little nervously. This was very different from a buggy ride in the Virginia countryside.

Finally they reached the village Martha had decided they should visit first. As soon as they entered the gate, a crowd of men and boys gathered around them. "Foreign devils," they said to one another in Chinese.

At Martha's command, the coolies put down the sedan chairs and helped the women out. Lottie rushed over to her sister. "Eddie, what are they saying?" she asked, looking at the gathering crowd.

"They're calling us foreign devils," Eddie replied, "but don't worry. That's the first thing they always say."

"And what else are they saying?" Lottie asked, frustrated that she was the only one who could not understand what was being said.

"Well," continued Eddie, "they're trying to decide whether we are men or women. They are confused because we're not wearing trousers like Chinese women."

"Oh," Lottie responded, looking down at what she had considered to be a perfectly feminine dress.

Edmonia pointed to a group that had gathered near a corner. "Look over there," she said. "There's a group of women we can talk to."

Lottie grabbed her sister's arm and started walking through the crowd of men toward the corner. As she did so, she questioned Eddie. "But I thought the women stayed inside their courtyards all the time."

"Well, that's true in the big cities like Tengchow, but in the villages, customs are much more relaxed. Most of these people are farmers, and they can't afford to hire someone to run errands for them."

Lottie nodded. By now she and Eddie were approaching the women, who stepped back into the shadow of a building as the missionary women came nearer.

"At least they didn't run away," Lottie whispered.

Finally several of the Chinese women plucked up their courage and began asking questions.

"What are they saying?" Lottie asked impatiently.

Eddie laughed. "They want to know all about you! They want to know if you are married and why your mother-in-law let you travel so far from your homeland without your husband."

"Oh," Lottie replied. "You can tell them I am a woman just like them, and that I have no husband. I came here to tell them some very important news about a God who loves them."

As Edmonia spoke to the women in Mandarin, the women fingered Lottie's silk dress and tugged gently on her ringlets.

"They certainly are curious, aren't they!" Lottie exclaimed to Eddie.

"You wait until we stop for lunch. We'll have quite an audience then," Edmonia responded.

"It's time to get organized," Martha called out, her booming voice cutting through the air. Lottie turned to look at her. Martha was carrying a large scroll that she quickly unraveled. On the scroll were the words in Mandarin to a Sunday school hymn titled "Happy Land."

"Hold this up, please," Martha instructed Lottie.

Lottie stood and held up the scroll while Martha and Sallie sang the song a couple of times. One by one the children joined in. They were fast learners. Martha picked out one child who had mastered all the words and gave him a copy of the hymn that had been hand copied onto red parchment. This stirred competition among the other children, who soon were all clamoring to show that they, too, had memorized the hymn.

The women stayed in the village for an hour or so, giving out red hymn sheets and talking to the women before moving on to the next village. They continued this pattern throughout the day. At one village, a very hostile man ordered them out of the area, and so the women moved on. And Eddie had been right; the easiest way to draw a crowd was to sit down and eat lunch. As they sat down for lunch, people of all ages crept closer and closer to the missionary women as they pulled objects from their picnic hamper. Everyone seemed particularly impressed with the forks the women used, as well as the napkin rings. Lottie felt like an exhibit at the zoo, but she was glad to see that the people of the surrounding villages did not appear to be frightened of them.

As she ate, Lottie thought of the meals she and Eddie had shared back at Viewmont. Their mother had always been particular about holding polite conversation and not staring at anyone else seated at the table. What would she have thought if she could have seen her two daughters eating lunch surrounded by a sea of curious brown faces? It was a long way from being pampered southern belles to being hardworking missionaries, but Lottie was sure her mother would have been proud of what her daughters were doing.

After lunch Sallie taught a hymn to all the people who had gathered to watch them eat, and then Martha talked to them for about twenty minutes. When the crowd grew restless, the women clambered back into their sedan chairs and moved on.

Lottie was exhausted and exhilarated by the time they arrived back in Tengchow that evening. She and three other women had single-handedly presented the gospel to hundreds of men and women who had never had the opportunity to hear it before. She could hardly wait for the next opportunity to get back out into the villages.

Chapter 8

Fallen Apart

"Lottie, I have to go! Help me pack," Eddie yelled as she burst into the upstairs bedroom the two sisters shared.

"What's wrong?" Lottie asked.

"Nothing's wrong. Something wonderful has happened. Here, read this." Edmonia thrust a piece of paper into Lottie's hand. The words on it were written in Mandarin, and Lottie could read only bits of it, but she was able to pick out the name of Mrs. Lan. Mrs. Lan was a member of the Monument Street Baptist Church, which Tarleton and Martha Crawford had started.

"Isn't it wonderful?" Edmonia smiled, throwing clothes into a cloth bag. "Mrs. Lan went back to the village where she grew up for the New Year's celebrations and started telling others about her faith. Now she has a huge crowd of people milling around the house where she was staying wanting to learn more. She has taught them all the hymns she knows and has read the Bible to them, and now she needs our help answering their questions. Sallie and I are leaving to go to the village at noon." Eddie hugged her sister. "Isn't it exciting?" she added, her eyes shining.

"Yes!" Lottie replied. "I wish I were going with you, but I guess someone needs to stay and help the Crawfords with the church."

Edmonia nodded. "I'll keep a journal and tell you all about it," she promised Lottie, pulling tight the drawstrings on her bag.

Two days later another letter arrived at the Crawfords' home, this time from Sallie Holmes. The letter said that so many people from the village were asking questions that the three women couldn't keep up with the demand. Sallie wondered whether there was some way Martha could send more missionaries to help them with the task.

Lottie watched as Martha tried to comprehend the predicament the women were in. Were there really so many questions that Mrs. Lan and the two missionaries couldn't answer them all? "This has never happened before!" she finally exclaimed. "It's astonishing. Tarleton and I have worked so long here and seen so few results." With tears in her eyes, she looked at Lottie. "We must go and see what we can do."

"Wonderful," replied Lottie, who had wanted to go with Edmonia from the beginning.

Martha persuaded the wife of a local Presbyterian missionary to go along as well. Soon the three of them were on their way to the village in sedan chairs.

What they found when they arrived at the village amazed them. A throng of Chinese people surrounded Mrs. Lan's house. Some of them were singing hymns quietly while others stood in small groups discussing who Jesus was and why He had come to earth.

Once their bags had been carried inside the house, the three women joined Edmonia, Sallie, and Mrs. Lan and went straight to work. They walked among the groups of people, answering their questions and showing them passages in the Bible that talked about Jesus and the gospel.

It was long after nightfall when the crowd finally drifted off to their own homes. At daybreak they were back again, eagerly waiting with a fresh round of questions to be answered. Lottie helped in any way she could, but once again she was frustrated by not being able to understand all that was being said.

After two days, a core group of new Christians had developed, and it was necessary to work out how to set up a church in the village. The other missionary women had to get back to their own responsibilities, and so it was decided that Eddie and Lottie should stay and organize the first-ever

Sunday service. As the other missionaries were leaving, Martha promised to send Mr. Mung, a deacon from Tengchow, to the village to preach the Sunday sermon.

The first Christian church service held in the village attracted a great deal of interest. As a result, Mrs. Lan and Mr. Mung agreed to stay on longer in the village to get the church properly established. Lottie and Edmonia promised that the other missionaries would take turns coming back for services, but for now it was time for the two sisters to get back to Tengchow. The new school year would soon be starting, and there was a lot of preparation to do.

It was a frigid Monday morning when Lottie and Eddie climbed into their open sedan chairs for the trip back to Tengchow. Lottie could not recall ever being so cold, not even when she had gone out in the middle of winter back at Viewmont. The wind whistled around her skirt, which she pulled tight around her legs. Lottie looked over to her sister and smiled. Eddie smiled back and waved. Nothing, not even the bitter cold, could take away the joy of the wonderful week that Lottie and Edmonia had shared. Things had worked out just as Lottie had hoped. Together they had proved that two single women were able to carry a full load of missionary work and do it well. What Lottie did not know was that this trip would mark the high point of Edmonia's missionary activities. As she rode along in her sedan chair, Edmonia was becoming ill with typhoid pneumonia.

By the time they reached Tengchow, Eddie needed to be helped out of the sedan chair and carried inside to her bed. Lottie became alarmed when Eddie did not get better quickly. It seemed to her that missionaries were failing all around them. The wife of one of the Presbyterian missionaries had died, leaving behind four small children, one of whom was a deaf mute. A missionary man had suffered a nervous breakdown. He sat staring at the wall until finally the mission agency sent someone to escort him home.

Trying to put her fears aside, Lottie nursed her sister as best she could. Finally she began to see small improvements in the condition of Edmonia's body, but not her mind. As she started to get better, Eddie became very angry and flew into uncontrollable rages over the smallest of things: a man carrying noisy chickens past her window, the soup that Lottie brought her being too cool, the letter she sent home several months before not yet being replied to. Anything and everything seemed to upset Edmonia.

Lottie had no idea how to help her sister. When school finally started up again, she tried to ease Edmonia's workload. Eddie did not actually teach the boys herself now but had hired and supervised a Chinese teacher to do that. Lottie soon found that this situation tried her patience. Although the teacher Eddie had hired knew he would be required to teach the Bible, he also smoked opium and twisted Christian teaching whenever he thought he could get away with it.

What also frustrated Lottie was that deep down she wanted to help the little girls of the town. In her opinion they had fewer opportunities than the boys. Girls were married off while they were still very young and sent to their new husband's home, where their mother-in-law took complete control over their life. Most girls could not read or write and had no knowledge of the world outside their town or village.

When she managed to get any spare time, Lottie loved to swim in the ocean or practice riding a donkey. She soon found that Sallie had been right: It was much easier to balance on a donkey than in a sedan chair. Lottie wrote many letters back home to her family and friends. She also kept in regular contact with Henry Allen Tupper, the secretary of the Southern Baptist Foreign Mission Board. Henry Tupper had been instrumental in both Edmonia's and Lottie's being given permission to go as single women missionaries to China. Henry Tupper made it a point to discuss Lottie's and Eddie's progress at every meeting of the Foreign Mission Board. In time, many Baptist women became interested in the Moon sisters' work. They were astonished that the two of them had given up a comfortable life in the South to serve in a strange and far-off country. Soon women's missionary societies were being formed in every church district, and they began looking for a project of their own.

Henry Tupper had just the project for them. Lottie had written asking his opinion on trying to raise money back home so that the Moon sisters could have a house of their own in Tengchow. Living with the Crawfords had become a trial. Tarleton Crawford was old and obstinate, and he seemed to annoy Edmonia at every turn. Much to Lottie's embarrassment, Eddie forgot all of her southern charm and responded with screaming and yelling. Lottie thought the work of the mission would go a lot more smoothly if the two were separated.

Several weeks later, an overjoyed Lottie received a letter from Henry Tupper telling her that instead of agreeing to the two thousand dollars she had suggested raising for a house, he had increased the amount to three thousand dollars. As soon as he had announced the goal of buying the Moon sisters a house, the women's missionary societies had taken up the challenge.

By the time the Southern Baptist Missions Convention of 1874 rolled around, twenty-five hundred dollars had been given toward the total cost of the house. Lottie was grateful. She and Edmonia decided to donate a quarter of their missionary allowance to make up the other five hundred dollars. Soon the three thousand dollars was waiting in a bank account in the United States for them to use.

The money was not needed right away, however. The wife of James Hartwell, who led the North Street Baptist Church in Tengchow, became ill, and the doctor advised James to take her back to the United States. As a result, the Hartwell home lay empty, and Lottie and Edmonia moved in. Lottie soon found she was able to get a lot more mission work done now that she didn't have to keep resolving arguments between Eddie and Tarleton Crawford.

By 1876 things were running as smoothly as could be expected. Lottie had taken over Edmonia's work supervising the boys school, and the number of students attending had risen to fourteen. Eddie spent much of her time in bed or around the house. She was constantly sick with influenza or asthma. Still, Lottie was glad to have her around, and when she was able, Eddie took care of running the house.

The missionaries in Tengchow took turns taking a short vacation to rest from their busy schedules. When Tarleton and Martha Crawford went to Japan in August, Edmonia, Lottie, and Sallie were the only Baptist missionaries left in the city. With great efficiency they took care of the school and handled Martha's duties as a nurse. Back in the United States, Henry Tupper was delighted to read how the three single women were coping so well without a man to "lean on."

When the Crawfords returned from Japan, it was Edmonia's turn to take a break. Everyone had advised her to spend the winter in Japan, as the climate there was milder and she was not coping well with the damp weather in Tengchow. Eddie met up with another woman missionary, Eliza Yates, in Shanghai, and together they journeyed to Nagasaki.

It was not a happy journey. Edmonia's nerves were raw, and she complained about everything.

Not only that, she seemed frightened and disoriented. Indeed, Eliza became so alarmed at Edmonia's behavior that she sent for Lottie. At the same time, she wrote to the Foreign Mission Board asking them to bring Edmonia Moon home, as she was not a well woman.

Lottie was shocked when she received Eliza's letter asking her to come to Japan. She had hoped that Eddie would feel better when she got to Japan, but apparently her health had gone downhill fast. Within hours of receiving the news, Sallie and Martha had worked out how to cover Lottie's workload between them so that Lottie could go to the aid of her sister. Soon Lottie was on her way to Shanghai to catch a ship that would take her across the Yellow Sea to Japan.

As she traveled, Lottie began to face the fact of Edmonia's physical and mental illness. In Tengchow, Lottie had sheltered her sister from people and carried most of Eddie's workload. But now Edmonia had gone out on her own and had fallen apart. Something more would have to be done about her condition.

The trip to Japan was uneventful, and when Lottie finally met up with Eddie, she was dismayed at how sick her sister was. Eliza had been right to send for her. There was no option but to take Edmonia back home to Virginia.

As Lottie crossed the Pacific Ocean by ship on her way home, hoping that Edmonia would survive the journey, she had no way of knowing that another sister, Mollie, was also very ill. The joyous family reunion Lottie had anticipated on her arrival home was tinged with the sad news that Mollie had died six weeks before. Mollie had left behind a husband and a baby daughter, Mamie.

Thankfully, the rest of the family were well and happy, and they were able to spend Christmas 1876 together at Viewmont, where Orie and her family were now living. It was almost like old times, though the family was not nearly as wealthy as it had been before the Civil War, and Lottie's mother was not there.

Orie took over care of Edmonia, prescribing for her bed rest along with large doses of whiskey and cod liver oil. That, along with the well-heated house, appeared to speed Edmonia's recovery.

The family was glad that Lottie had brought her sister home. It was obvious to all that Eddie had suffered some kind of breakdown and would never be fit to go back to China. However, many Southern Baptists were not so forgiving of the Moon sisters or the three other missionaries who had returned home from China at about the same time. Many of these people could see no reason why Lottie, the other three people, or even Edmonia had to come home. After all, they had pledged to stay in China until death. Why had they given up so easily?

Easily? Lottie fumed! She was appalled by their attitude. These people had no idea how difficult or dangerous it was to live in China. As a result, she traveled whenever she could to speak to Baptist groups about the hard conditions in China. She quickly discovered, though, that it was often more effective to write letters to people and churches describing missionary life. She wrote about all the missionaries and their children who had died in China, about the dreadful diseases that were so easily contracted there, about the violence of local militias toward missionaries, and about the stress of living in a totally foreign environment. She encouraged the mission board to be a little more understanding of its missionaries. Indeed, Lottie felt as passionate about educating Baptists concerning the realities of missionary life as she did educating Chinese people about the Christian life. Everywhere she went she challenged American Christians to become more supportive of missionaries regardless of where they served. Otherwise the whole world would not get to hear the gospel.

Perhaps it was because of Lottie's education and her experiences as a missionary, but people began to listen to what she had to say. Mission boards started to ask questions about whether missionaries ought to be able to come home every eight or ten years and whether more attention ought to be paid to providing better housing for them.

Lottie was very pleased that her visit had stirred up such questions, but what she wanted most was to get back "home" to China. Returning to the mission field was not easy, though, as the foreign missions budget had been slashed since she arrived back in the United States. However, Lottie still had access to the Moon housing fund, which had never been used. She asked the contributors to the fund if they would allow the money to be spent on her passage back to China. The donors immediately agreed. What use was a house if there was no missionary to live in it?

It was November 8, 1877, almost exactly a year since she had left China, that Lottie Moon climbed aboard the *Tokio Maru* in San Francisco. This time she was no longer the novice missionary among the other thirteen missionaries aboard on their way to serve in Japan and China.

After her arrival back in Shanghai, Lottie spent several days visiting with friends there. One person she visited was Anna Safford, her old teaching companion from the female academy in Danville, Kentucky, and the girls school in Cartersville, Georgia. Anna now lived and worked in Soochow, a village just outside Shanghai. The two women enjoyed a wonderful time together, reminiscing and sharing about each other's missionary work. All too soon, though, it was time for Lottie to make her way back to Tengchow.

Chapter 9

Heavenly People

"Welcome back, Miss Moon," yelled several of the schoolboys who were waiting outside the Hartwells' house for Lottie. Lottie had finally made it back to Tengchow, a year to the day since she had been reunited with her family at Viewmont. As she thought about it, Lottie realized that the Chinese Christians at Monument Street Church and the children in the school were also her family, and they were a family in need.

In the year Lottie had been away, famine had broken out in the region, and many peasants were starving to death. Lottie saw them everywhere—in the streets, begging at the market, and clamoring to get into the church to warm themselves. The famine presented a unique opportunity for the Christians in Tengchow, and Lottie was pleased to learn they had taken offerings for the poor and given away a lot of food to the hungry.

Other changes had taken place at Tengchow, too. Sallie Holmes had faced the heart-wrenching decision of whether to return to the United States with her son, Landrum, to help him settle into college or send him off alone and continue her missionary work. Eventually she chose to stay at her post in Tengchow, but the decision did not come without tears over being separated from her only child. And while Sallie had lost a son, Martha Crawford now had two children, ages fourteen and seven. The children's parents had been missionaries in Japan but had both died, leaving the children orphaned. The Crawfords had adopted them.

On the voyage back to China, Lottie had decided it was time to pursue the dream of a school for girls. As soon as she arrived back, she set about making the dream a reality. Finding a building to house the school was not difficult; a row of rooms was attached to the Hartwells' house that could be used for that purpose. However, finding students to attend classes proved nearly impossible. Girls in China had few choices that they could make about their lives, which proved to be the problem in getting them to school. Girls had no choice, for instance, about having their feet bound when they were four or five years old. Traditionally, in China, small feet were seen as a sign of beauty, and no man would marry a woman with unbound feet. But bound feet were quite a problem when it came to going to school. They had to be rebandaged often, and they easily became infected, which sometimes led to a girl's death.

Another choice that girls lacked was whom to marry. Sometimes at birth Chinese girls were promised to future husbands. Of course, they didn't get married right then, but they were expected to be ready to go whenever their future mother-in-law decided it was time for the wedding. If a girl was away at school, she wouldn't be ready to go immediately to be with her husband and his family. And because most girls were promised to be somebody's wife, no one could see any point in educating them. Why would a girl, or any woman for that matter, need to know how to read or write when her main duties would be to clean house, cook meals, and rear children under the watchful eye of her mother-in-law?

For all of these reasons it was very difficult to get girls to attend school. Yet Lottie would not give up on the idea. "I have to start somewhere," she told herself as she scoured the countryside looking for prospective students.

After two months of searching, Lottie returned to Tengchow in February 1878, having persuaded five girls to attend her school. The girls were not the daughters of high-class Chinese families she had hoped to attract. In fact, most of them were fleeing a life of prostitution or parents who spent all the family money on opium or gambling. Despite this, Lottie was sure she could teach them.

Before the year was over, school enrollment had swelled to thirteen girls. Since no one would pay for his daughter to attend school, Lottie was forced to assume responsibility for the girls' housing, food, and medicine. However, she was glad to do it. She firmly believed that somewhere in the hearts of these often willful and unruly girls were the seeds of tomorrow's Christian women.

Lottie combined American and Chinese ways of teaching the girls. As she had done for her American students, Lottie gave the girls singing lessons and read them Bible stories. But there was no changing the way they learned from books. The normal Chinese method was to be able to recite huge chunks of text by heart, and the girls soon set about learning the entire Gospel of Matthew. They would stand with their backs to Lottie, yelling out verse after verse until they could recite the whole twenty-eight chapters of the Gospel straight through.

While the girls school kept her busy, Lottie tried not to miss an opportunity to go with Sallie Holmes out into the countryside to share the gospel message. One winter day in 1878, a year after Lottie had returned from the United States, Sallie sent word by messenger that she was taking a trip into the countryside and wanted Lottie to join her.

Lottie stood peering past the messenger at the icy weather conditions. It didn't seem to her like the best weather to be out in the countryside. "Tell Miss Holmes I think we should wait until the storm passes," she told the messenger.

Half an hour later, Lottie received a knock at the door. It was the same messenger with a note for her. On the note was one word: "Go." Lottie sighed. Traveling in the countryside was difficult enough when the weather was fine, but it was almost unbearable in winter when icy winds and rain blew in off the ocean. There was nothing appealing to Lottie about standing in freezing rain while being called a foreign devil or being refused entrance to an inn for the night. Still, if Sallie was willing to brave such weather, Lottie would accompany her.

Lottie padded herself with extra layers of flannel petticoats and wrapped some cold noodles and chicken to eat along the way. Soon the two women set out in sedan chairs, the wind whipping around their legs. They reached the first village and stood in the street waiting to attract attention. It came in the form of a young boy Lottie had given a Gospel of Mark to on a previous visit. The boy held the tract up and grinned at them.

Lottie smiled back and began asking the boy questions about what he had read. Soon another boy joined him, and then an older woman and two little girls. The woman stroked Lottie's sleeve while the little girls giggled and tried to lift up her dress to see her petticoat.

As much as Lottie wanted to swat them away, she waited until they had satisfied their curiosity. Then the woman started in with the inevitable questions. "How old are you? Do you have children or are you barren? Why does your mother-in-law allow you to go out alone?"

Lottie tried to answer each question graciously, though it was still difficult for her to accept strangers touching her and asking her personal questions—questions no polite person in southern society would dream of asking.

Nightfall came early in the winter, and just as the two missionary women were deciding it was time to travel on, one of their chair bearers announced he had relatives in the village who were prepared to shelter them both for the night. A family willing to have foreign devils in their house? Lottie was delighted. She knew it was a brave step for an uneducated Chinese person to take. So many outrageous rumors were circulating about foreigners that most families would not be able to sleep if they knew a "devil" was in their house. Lottie had heard many of these rumors, which never ceased to amaze her. People had seen missionaries eating pickled onions and reported that they were eating the eyeballs of small children. They had seen children's porcelain dolls and pronounced them to be embalmed babies, and men drinking red currant juice were said to be drinking the blood of murdered children.

When the women arrived at their host's house, they found the entire neighborhood was waiting for them. Immediately the questions started up. Sallie took charge of the situation and invited the boys to join her in the yard while Lottie took charge of the girls and women in the house. Because of the way Chinese society worked, there was no way the men could be seen learning from a woman, but Lottie noticed a group of men forming at the gate. She knew the men would stand there and listen to Sallie talking to the young boys without officially joining in.

Lottie walked into the low-roofed house and looked around. The side room where she and Sallie were to stay was only about nine feet square, and most of that space was taken up by the *k'ang,* the knee-high platform that served as a bed. This k'ang, Lottie observed, was not made of bricks, like most, but was made of dried mud. A tiny worn mat covered the k'ang. It was all the bedding the women would be offered for the night. The floor of the room was packed dirt, and there was a paper-covered window in the far wall, but no door, just an opening to the rest of the house. Everything in the house was covered in a thick, grimy film created by the smoke of many generations of inhabitants.

"Do you have heavenly books?" asked one of the girls who had squeezed past Lottie to sit on the k'ang.

"Yes, let me read to you," Lottie said, amazed that by now about fifteen people had squeezed themselves onto the k'ang waiting to hear what she had to say.

Time passed quickly, and the women asked Lottie question after question about Christianity until she was too hoarse to speak anymore. Only then did they let her alone. However, they all promised to be back first thing in the morning.

After the women left, Lottie, totally exhausted, unlaced her shoes and fell onto the mat on the k'ang fully clothed. She was asleep in no time. The noise of scratching chickens awoke her early the next morning. She peered out the open doorway into the family room. Fifteen sets of eyes peered back. Lottie tried to smile, but she was weary of being watched every moment. She dreaded the next volley of questions that was sure to be unleashed as soon as she left the bedroom.

Sure enough, as she walked into the family room, more people flooded in from outside. "Look how untidy her hair is," said one girl. "Oh, and did you see the way she put the rope through the holes in her shoes?" asked another. There was a general rumbling of interest, and everyone looked down at Lottie's shoes.

Soon Sallie, who had been sleeping on the k'ang beside Lottie, emerged from the bedroom. The two missionary women sat down and ate a breakfast of millet. Four small boys stood staring down at them while they ate. Lottie watched as people outside ripped the paper out of the window for a better view of the women eating.

"I've counted them," Sallie said in English. "There are thirty people watching us!"

"Thirty!" Lottie echoed in Chinese.

Their hostess must have guessed what Sallie had said. "I am so sorry. I beg your humble pardon, but you must forgive all the viewers. You see, we have never seen any heavenly people before," the woman apologized.

Lottie forced herself to smile again and nodded her head. "Let them look," she said, "and when we have finished eating, we will tell them more about the heavenly book."

The day was as busy as the one before had been. Hundreds of people reached out to touch Lottie's skin or her clothes, and she was asked the same old questions time after time. As the day wore on, the words of their hostess kept playing over in Lottie's mind: We have never seen any heavenly people before.

Lottie thought a lot about the opportunities she had to share the gospel message with people who had never heard it before. This was what she had come to China to do. At the same time, it had proved to be more difficult than she had imagined it would be, especially being endlessly watched and touched and asked questions. She liked her privacy and had been raised to believe there were certain questions you didn't ask people. However, the Chinese valued none of this. Lottie decided as they headed back to Tengchow that it was time to overcome her discomfort at being observed so closely. She wanted to be more like Sallie, who took it all in stride and didn't become frustrated at being watched all the time.

When Lottie arrived home she wrote in her diary, "I must conquer my unwillingness to talk and be fingered, and teach the children."

A copy of the Baptist newspaper the *Biblical Recorder* was waiting for Lottie when she arrived home. Normally, Lottie loved to read it, but this particular issue made her angry. One of the front-page articles announced that "in this modern world we are at the end of the days of missionary hardship."

Lottie wished the writer of the article could have been on her last trip. She was frustrated that Christians back home did not understand the hardships that not only she personally but also all missionaries had to endure. Sallie had sent her son home to college and now had the worry of not having heard of his whereabouts for over a year. And her own sister, Edmonia, had been unable to take the strain of life in China. Lottie felt something had to be said on behalf of all missionaries, and she was the person to say it.

The next day Lottie took out a pen and some paper and wrote a long letter to the editor of the *Biblical Recorder* complaining about the article. Afterward she wrote to her old friend Henry Tupper and told him: "I am always ashamed to dwell on physical hardships. But, this time I have departed from my usual reticence because I know that there are some who, in their pleasant homes in America without any real knowledge of the facts, declare that the days of missionary hardships are over. To speak in the open air in a foreign tongue from six to eleven times a day is no trifle. The fatigue of travel is something.... If anyone fancies sleeping on brick beds in rooms with dirt floors and walls blackened by the smoke of many generations, the yard also being the stable yard and the stable itself being within three feet of your door, I wish to declare most emphatically that as a matter of taste, I differ.... I find it most unpleasant. If anyone thinks that the constant risk of exposure to smallpox and other contagious disease, against which the Chinese take no precaution whatever, is just the most charming thing in life, I shall continue to differ. In a word, let him try it! A few days of roughing it as we ladies do habitually will convince the most skeptical."

Lottie hoped these words would lay to rest any idea among Christians back in the United States that there were no longer any hardships to be endured by missionaries serving in foreign lands.

Chapter 10

Mission Stations

"Is it any wonder that we feel like kings' daughters tonight?" Lottie wrote in her journal. "There are beautiful spiderwebs on the rafters and clean matting on the k'ang.... With a heart full of joy, it is no effort to speak to the people."

Lottie put down her pen and smiled. Finally she had come to terms with her surroundings. The joy of telling others about her faith had conquered her worries about hygiene, illness, and bugs. She now felt at home among some of the poorest people on earth.

Just as Lottie was finding her niche as a missionary, however, Tarleton Crawford was losing his grip on reality. His wife confided in Lottie that he was experiencing "brain trouble." It was obvious to Lottie that he was suffering a nervous breakdown similar to the kind that Edmonia had suffered. Soon afterward, Tarleton Crawford packed a bag and left Tengchow in the middle of the night, alone and without any money. Martha Crawford was distraught and waited anxiously for some word of his whereabouts. Finally word came that he had made his way back to the United States.

Lottie knew that Tarleton Crawford's life had been difficult in Tengchow, but she partly blamed the Foreign Mission Board for his breakdown. In their nearly twenty-five years of missionary service in China, the Crawfords had never been allowed to return home on furlough. All they had been allowed was one short vacation to Japan. Was it any wonder that Tarleton Crawford had fled back to the United States for a break?

Lottie was convinced that the Southern Baptists could do a much better job helping their missionaries stay healthy in body and mind while on the mission field. Current mission policies needed to be reformed to reflect the realities a missionary faced every day. When she accompanied Edmonia home, Lottie had raised the issue with the Foreign Mission Board of missionaries being allowed to take a furlough. She decided it was now time to once again stir up the board over the issue. She knew that change would not happen overnight, and she was prepared to keep pushing, even if it took a lifetime.

Again Lottie resorted to paper and pen. She fired off her first volley, a letter to the Foreign Mission

Board urging it to consider furloughs for missionaries rather than sending them out for life and making them feel like second-class Christians if their health failed and they had to return home. In her letter she wrote, "It is as if you were saying to a soldier you were sending to the front, 'Do battle with the enemy. Mind, no furloughs! We expect you to fall on the field.' "

While she waited for a response to her letter, Lottie became busier than ever. Now that Tarleton Crawford was gone, Lottie, Martha Crawford, and Sallie Holmes had taken over his work responsibilities in addition to their own. Things soon got worse. Sallie, who still had not heard anything from her son, Landrum, spent much of her time in a daze wondering whether he was dead or so busy at school that he had forgotten to contact his mother. Not knowing was causing Sallie to become more and more depressed. In the end, she could barely get out of bed each morning, and with great regret, Lottie arranged for her to be sent home. Sallie left Tengchow in August 1881. It was a sad day for Lottie. The two women had become close friends. Sallie had taught Lottie much about Chinese culture and how to relate to the people.

Sallie's departure left only two Baptist women in all of North China, and Lottie felt keenly the weight of trying to do everything. At first she and Martha divided the workload between them, but before long, Lottie came to the conclusion that they desperately needed more workers. She wrote another of her stirring letters to the Foreign Mission Board pointing out that they now had only two missionaries working among the three million people in the region.

Before the year was over, they received at least one more worker. Tarleton Crawford returned from his roaming, looking a little better physically. However, he was very critical and rude to everyone, especially his wife. Indeed, it wasn't too long before Martha Crawford herself began to have a breakdown, and she returned to the United States for a break, leaving Tarleton and Lottie to battle on with the work.

Lottie sent out more pleas for helpers, and finally in January 1882, two single men, Weston Halcomb and Cicero Pruitt, were sent to answer the call. Lottie was overjoyed. They were the first new missionary faces she had seen since her arrival in China nearly nine years before. She was even more pleased when she discovered the two young men were natural evangelists, eager to go with her into the villages to preach. They both learned quickly, and soon Lottie had them talking to the men while she talked to the women and children.

Ida Tiffany joined the group, too. She was a Presbyterian missionary who had sailed from the United States with Weston and Cicero. Ida, whom Lottie liked a great deal, and Cicero had fallen in love on the voyage, and Ida had decided to become a Baptist. The two of them were married soon after they arrived.

As far as Lottie was concerned, things were looking up. Young people, both men and women, were coming forward to fill the missionary ranks.

By now Lottie had moved into Sallie Holmes's old compound. The compound consisted of three 300-year-old houses that were surrounded by a common wall. The houses in the compound were simple, with paper windows and dirt floors, but Lottie made them into a comfortable home and a place to host the new missionaries while they adjusted to the local culture. The place soon became known as the "Little Crossroads."

The year 1883 brought more changes. Lottie's girls school had been going well, but in the spring, a serious outbreak of disease swept across the region, and the girls were sent home with the hope that their lives would be spared from the ravages of the illness. While the girls were gone, Lottie thought a lot about what she really wanted to do in China. Although the school had produced some good results, Lottie could not stop thinking about all the illiterate women in the villages who needed to hear the gospel. Every day she longed to be in the villages, especially now that she had two young missionary men to talk to the men. She began to dream of a long chain of mission stations stretching from one end of Shantung province to the other. Instead of reopening the girls school, which influenced about thirty girls and their families, Lottie decided to concentrate fully on her work among the villages.

Lottie also received some sad news from home. Her sister, Dr. Orianna Andrews, had died after becoming sick with cancer. She left behind her husband and six sons. She had actually given birth to twelve sons in the course of her life, but six of them had died in infancy. Lottie worried about how Edmonia would take the news. In her letters Eddie often sounded depressed.

In 1884 another resident came to live at the Little Crossroads. Mattie Roberts had been sent out by the mission board to be Lottie's assistant. Lottie was glad to have another single woman working with her. It had been three years since Sallie Holmes had left. However, the situation didn't last long. Weston Halcomb began to pay attention to Mattie Roberts. Soon the two were married, and Lottie was in need of another assistant.

At the same time, the Southern Baptist missionaries in Tengchow decided it was time to put their new plan into action. They headed out to staff the chain of mission stations that Lottie had dreamed about across Shantung province. The Pruitts and the Halcombs set out for Hwanghsien, a village about 120 miles from Tengchow. The next step in the plan called for Lottie to move farther south to the town of P'ingtu. Before she could leave, however, Ida Pruitt became ill, and Lottie went to Hwanghsien to nurse her. Sadly, the young missionary bride who had arrived with such high hopes two years before died. Her death made forty-four-year-old Lottie even more determined to make a difference in China with however much of her life was left.

In December 1885, Lottie finally headed south to P'ingtu, a town far from the safety and authority of the treaty ports that had been set up to protect foreigners in China. She set off in a shentze, bracing herself for the journey ahead. She was the first Southern Baptist woman ever to be given permission to open up a new mission station alone, and she was determined to do her best. She also knew she was going into dangerous land. There were no other foreigners in P'ingtu. In fact, a Presbyterian missionary had lived there for a while, but he had been unable to adjust to living so far from other Westerners and had asked to be sent back to a coastal port. The people of P'ingtu had never seen a white woman before, and Lottie knew this would mean another round of questions, prodding, and poking for her. But she was ready to face whatever lay ahead.

Following the shentze was a caravan of mules carrying Lottie's belongings. Lottie had thought long and hard about what to take with her, knowing she would not have access to anything European until the summer, when she had promised to return to Tengchow for a visit. Eventually she had decided to take her own bedding and mattress to make the k'ang more comfortable, some Greek and Latin books to keep her mind stimulated, flour, sugar, coffee, and a large supply of Chinese gospel tracts and hymnbooks. The tracts and hymnals were packed into a wooden trunk that two of the mules carried slung between them. The trunk would serve as a table, the only piece of furniture Lottie would have once she arrived in P'ingtu.

Also traveling with Lottie were Mr. and Mrs. Chao, two Christians from Tengchow who had volunteered to help her set up the new mission station.

Lottie had divided the trip into four days of traveling thirty miles each day. Nights on the journey were spent staying in some of the worst inns Lottie had ever seen. Rats ran around her feet, and ticks and lice crawled all over her body. By the first morning, Lottie had scratched her skin raw.

By the time the caravan of donkeys and shentzes reached its destination, everyone was sore and bruised. After their arrival, Mr. Chao set out to find a home for them to live in. He came back an hour later with a broad smile on his face. "I found my cousin, Chao Teh Shin. He has a house on the western side of town and is willing to rent it to you for twenty-four dollars a year."

"Did you see the house?" Lottie asked.

"I have just come from there," Mr. Chao replied. "I think you will like it. There are four rooms in a row."

Lottie nodded. "Can we go back and look at it together?" she inquired, thinking the house sounded like a hopeful lead.

And it was. The house was very simple, mud brick on the outside, with a thatched roof and paper windows and dirt floors and smoke-blackened walls inside, but Lottie liked it right away. It looked to be in good repair with no telltale water stains on the rafters, and it was in a bustling part of town.

"I'll take it," Lottie said, already thinking of how to turn the empty house into a home. The last room on the left had the k'ang in it. "We'll use this room as the meeting room during the day, and I'll sleep here at night," she said as she motioned for one of the coolies to bring in her mattress and bedding. "The next room must be the kitchen, of course," she continued, eyeing the hole where the heat from the stove would go to heat the airspace under the k'ang. Like most Chinese homes, the house had been rented without a stove, and soon Lottie had coolies unloading the stove she had brought with her. She decided the last two rooms would be a storeroom and an entryway. The Chaos arranged to stay nearby at another cousin's house.

Within a couple of days Lottie had everything set up the way she wanted it. Fresh straw covered the dirt floor, pale blue paper covered the blackened walls, and her trunk was set up beside the k'ang to serve as a table.

Once everything was taken care of, Lottie sat and waited. She did not go out into the streets and preach or go visiting her neighbors. This time she had a new strategy. She had decided that missionaries often made a big impression when they went out into the streets, but they did not make many friends. Instead, Lottie decided to stay at home and wait for the curious residents of P'ingtu to come to her.

To aid her in this process, Lottie had a "secret weapon": sugar cookies! The people in this part of China did not have flour made from wheat, but Lottie had brought six 20-pound sacks with her. She decided to use some of the flour to make cookies for the neighborhood children. Back in Virginia, no child could resist the offer of a freshly baked cookie, and Lottie suspected children in P'ingtu would be no different. As soon as the stove was properly installed, she set about making her first batch of sugar cookies. When they were cooked, she put them on a plate and walked outside her new house. As she did so, hands reached out to touch her clothing, and an old woman poked her arm.

"Would you like to try a cookie?" Lottie politely asked the people around her.

The crowd shrunk back, as if Lottie were offering them a poisonous potion. Finally, after some soothing talk, one little boy darted forward and grabbed a cookie. Soon he was licking his lips for the last crumb, and several other boys gathered up the courage to take a cookie for themselves. When all the cookies were gone, Lottie went back inside. She smiled to herself. Everything was going according to plan. If she was not mistaken, visitors would start coming to the house soon.

Sure enough, as she predicted, it wasn't long before someone plucked up the courage to visit Lottie. It was the wife of the owner of the house, and she came asking to be Lottie's laundress. Lottie agreed, and together they sat and talked and drank coffee, the one American luxury Lottie allowed herself. The next visitor was a man who wanted a job drawing water from the well for her. It was agreed that each day at sunrise he would deliver two buckets to the back door.

Within several days, Lottie had a steady stream of visitors to her new house. She was very pleased about how well her plan was working out. She wrote home in a letter, "We need to make friends before we can hope to make converts."

When Lottie did go out, she took Mrs. Chao with her. Mrs. Chao introduced her to family members and friends, and through this quiet approach, Lottie was invited to speak to many people in their homes. Still, there were those who taunted her and called her a foreign devil. This time Lottie had made up her mind not to tolerate such behavior. If a child called her a foreign devil, she took the boy or girl to his or her mother and asked that the child be taught good manners. If a woman goaded her, she would turn and retort, "Do not call me a devil. We are both women, and we both come from a common ancestor. If I am a devil, what does that make you?" With this approach, slowly the attitude of the taunters began to change.

Something Lottie had not predicted helped her to become even more accepted in P'ingtu. Lottie had always thought that Western missionaries who dressed like the Chinese looked silly. She had even written articles for the *Religious Herald* stating as much. However, as winter arrived, Lottie was surprised by just how cold it got. She piled on two layers of flannel petticoats, her woolen day dress, and a thick shawl. Still the beating snow on the thatched roof chilled her to the bone. In desperation, she paid a neighbor to make her a Chinese-style jacket. Lottie was very pleased with the jacket, which was heavily padded and went nearly to the floor. More important, it kept her warm, much warmer than she would have predicted. Next she ordered a dark blue robe with foot-wide sleeves and black satin binding. She wore this over everything else she had on, like a huge overcoat. Once again Lottie was amazed at how much warmer she felt wearing the robe, so warm, in fact, that she didn't take it off for weeks.

As soon as she went outside in her new garb, Lottie realized what a difference wearing it made. When she slicked her long black hair back in a bun, many people who passed her didn't even realize she was a foreigner. And those who did recognize her were much friendlier. Lottie could see she had made a mistake in her stand against wearing Chinese clothing. Far from being silly, such clothing was helping her to become an accepted member of the town.

Lottie also found that her new wardrobe had another benefit. She now wore so many layers of clothing it was like walking around with pillows strapped to her body. When she made trips out into the surrounding villages, she hardly felt the bumps of the donkeys and the shentze!

Chapter 11

The Jesus Way

It is a small house just outside of Scottsville, with only four rooms, but I have outfitted it with new Victorian furniture. I have called it Bonheur." Lottie read the letter written in her sister's neatly sloping handwriting three times, trying to picture the little house Edmonia had bought for both of them. The sisters had received the money to buy the house when the last parcel of Viewmont land was sold off. Life at Viewmont seemed such a long time ago to Lottie. For a moment she thought about the picnics the family had on the lawn, with servants to anticipate their every need, and the dinner parties shared with neighbors where the conversation about politics and Greek literature and French art was always stimulating. It was as though it had all existed in another lifetime for Lottie. The genteel southern lifestyle of her youth was very far removed from the realities of living in China.

Lottie was sitting at her desk in the Little Crossroads in Tengchow when she read the letter. She had come back to Tengchow for a summer break. The summer temperature in P'ingtu was over one hundred degrees. The heat, mixed with stifling humidity, could quickly sap one's strength, and to avoid that, Lottie had sought the more temperate coastal climate found in Tengchow. As well, Lottie had become desperately lonely in P'ingtu. She had to find someone to talk to in English before she forgot the language!

Her break so far was proving to be as much work as P'ingtu. As usual, there was far more to do than there were workers to do it. To make matters worse, a new Baptist missionary, Enos Davault, had died after battling "heart paralysis," a polite way of saying he suffered physical problems as a result of a mental and emotional breakdown. The Davaults and the Joiners had been sent by the Foreign Mission Board to help staff the new mission stations that had been opened in Shantung province. Both families had been based in Hwanghsien. While her husband was ill, Enos's wife, weak from giving birth and unable to adjust to the harsh climate of the area, took the baby and headed to southern China where the climate was more agreeable. However, she had not been able to adjust to the climate or the living conditions there and eventually returned to the United States.

At the same time, the Joiners had also left for the United States. The Southern Baptist Foreign Mission Board had understood that James Joiner needed a break from conditions in China, and so they had sent him to Siberia. For some reason Lottie could not fathom, the board considered Siberia a good place to recuperate! When James returned from there he was in worse shape than before he left, and the board had no choice but to recall him to the United States before he, too, was overcome with heart paralysis.

Lottie sat and thought about the new Baptist missionaries who had joined her on the mission field during her fourteen years in China. There had been eight of them in all, and of those eight, three—Enos Davault, Ida Pruitt, and Mattie Halcomb—had died. Three of them, the Joiners and Enos Davault's widow, had returned permanently to the United States. One, Weston Halcomb, had resigned from the mission and now worked for the U.S. consulate in Chefoo. Only one of the eight missionaries, Cicero Pruitt, remained at his post.

Lottie placed her face in her hands. What could she say in her letter home to the Foreign Mission Board? Even though the Southern Baptists had only one worker left out of the eight they had sent, they needed to send more, and more money as well. Lottie knew that the constant worry of the missionaries as to whether the board would have the money to meet the budget and pay their salary added greatly to the stress they felt in an already difficult situation.

Something was about to change among the Southern Baptists back home, however, that would greatly improve missionary life for Lottie and the other Baptist missionaries. The women in Southern Baptist churches had been meeting together for a number of years to encourage missions. They had formed small local mission societies and groups within their churches, but they had never banded together and been given "official" recognition from the powerful Southern Baptist Convention. In May 1887, women from many of these churches met together and decided it was time they had an official voice. With the help of many influential pastors, they pushed the issue until a resolution was passed to link the groups and recognize them as the Woman's Missionary Union.

At the same time, Lottie had been inspired by a practice she had heard the Methodist women were following. The week before Christmas, the women encouraged all Methodists to pray and then give money to missions. Lottie, who noted that the Methodists took much better care of their missionaries, wondered why the Southern Baptists couldn't do the same thing. She wrote a letter to the *Foreign Mission Journal* suggesting the church take up such an offering during Christmas 1887. The letter began, "I wonder how many of us really believe that it is more blessed to give than to receive?" Baptist women, feeling newly empowered by their official recognition, were looking for a cause to get behind, and they eagerly seized on the idea of a Christmas offering as a rallying point.

Lottie was thrilled to learn of this turn of events, though she would not hear about the eventual results of the offering suggestion for some time. She was on her way back to P'ingtu, where she received no mail at all. It had not been an easy decision to return there in the fall of 1887. Lottie was feeling weary, and amazingly, the Foreign Mission Board had approved a one-year furlough for her. Even though her throat hurt constantly from talking for up to fourteen hours a day and she longed to see her sister, Lottie was not yet ready to go home. Too much work still had to be done, and there was no one else to do it.

Before the mule train arrived to take her "home" to P'ingtu, Lottie wrote to the Foreign Mission Board telling them she would try to "hold on to next June [1888] if I find that my health justifies it. I have an intense horror of going home 'broken down,' to be of no use to myself or anybody else."

As she wrote these words, she was thinking of James Joiner, who had gone home quite deranged. Lottie would rather not go home at all than go home in such a state. Her hope was that she could survive another year alone. She had no idea of the wonderful adventure that lay ahead.

Lottie had been back in P'ingtu only a week when three men visited her. They did not knock on the door (no one did). Instead, they walked right into Lottie's house. Lottie offered them cookies and coffee and asked what they wanted.

"We have come on behalf of Dan Ho-bang," said the man with the longest mustache. "We are from

Sha-ling, and we have been sent to bring you back with us to teach us all the Jesus way."

"You have?" Lottie replied. "And what do you know of the Jesus way?" she inquired.

"Not much, but Dan Ho-bang wants us to know more," the man responded eagerly. "He came back from Hwanghsien, where he heard a man say that Jesus could remove our sins from us. Is that true?"

"Yes, it is," Lottie answered.

"Then we have a shentze waiting outside the door to take you back with us."

Lottie nodded. If Dan Ho-bang had gone to so much trouble to invite a foreign woman to speak with him, she was ready to go.

Sha-ling was ten miles from P'ingtu, and Lottie prayed the entire way there. She hoped there would be serious inquirers waiting when she arrived.

As the procession entered the small village of about fifty families, many people rushed out to meet Lottie.

"It is the lady with the heavenly book!" exclaimed one man.

"Yes, and she will tell us how our sins may be evaporated!" shouted another man, waving wildly at Lottie.

Soon the shentze came to a halt in front of a low gray house. A man came out to meet Lottie and bowed. "I am Dan Ho-bang, and I thank you for coming to my humble home. Please come in and have tea with us, and then would you be so kind as to answer our questions about the Jesus way?"

"Thank you," Lottie replied, wondering how she was going to handle the situation. Both Chinese tradition and her own Baptist upbringing made it difficult for her to imagine talking directly to the men, yet they were the ones asking questions. What was she to do?

As she sipped steaming hot tea, Lottie looked around the room and came up with an idea. "Do you have some way to divide the room so the women can listen to what I have to say as well as the men? The Jesus way is for both men and women equally," she said.

Dan Ho-bang looked astonished. "You would teach our women the way?" he asked.

"Yes," Lottie replied, "but I do not teach the men and the women in the same room. It would not be proper."

Dan Ho-bang's wife, Peling, spoke up. "I could weave a screen out of cornstalks," she volunteered, pouring more tea for Lottie.

"Thank you," Lottie said. "Tell anyone who wants to hear that I will explain the Jesus way tonight."

Lottie spent the rest of the day preparing for the meeting. As soon as it got dark, Peling brought out dishes filled with bean oil. She floated wicks in the dishes to make candles. Dan Ho-bang brought the screen inside and positioned it across the room, and Lottie hung up her hymn banner. Soon everything was ready. All they needed now were the people.

Soon people began to stream into the house until there was barely enough room to sit. The men were on one side on the k'ang, the women and children were on the other side sitting on the dirt floor, and the screen divided the two groups. The women pushed their children to the front of the room close to Lottie, saying, "They will learn more quickly, and then they can teach us when you are gone."

Lottie stood on the women's side of the room and started to sing a hymn. She began with "Jesus Loves Me," and she stopped after every line to explain its meaning. Then she invited the crowd to join in. They were very off-key, but Lottie was not worried. In fact, she was thrilled. Here was a group of people who were trying to grasp God's love for them for the very first time.

Next Lottie taught the crowd a short prayer and read a passage from the Gospel of Matthew. The evening flew by, but no one wanted to go home. Long into the night the men and women shouted out questions, which Lottie did her best to answer. The crowd left the house only when Lottie was too hoarse to speak anymore.

The crowd the next night was even larger, and larger still the night after that. There was no more room in Dan Ho-bang's house, so Lottie moved the meeting to an empty warehouse. She also sent a messenger back to Tengchow to fetch Martha Crawford, who had returned from furlough. Lottie needed help fast.

Thankfully, Martha came right away and set to work helping Lottie. Interest continued to grow in the Jesus way until twenty of the fifty families in

Sha-ling were coming to hear Lottie and Martha every night and on Sunday mornings as well. There was too much work for two women to handle, so they called for Cicero Pruitt to come and help. Cicero came quickly, which relieved Lottie, as he could sit with the men and answer their questions directly.

Cicero had good news to tell Lottie. He had met a charming young Presbyterian missionary named Anna Seward, and they were going to be married early in the new year. Lottie was delighted. Once again there would be another American woman within one hundred miles of P'ingtu.

Eventually a new church in Sha-ling began to organize. Church members became distraught, however, when they learned that Lottie would be returning to Tengchow for a summer break and the Foreign Mission Board had not appointed anyone to replace her. Several of the new converts wrote letters to the board. One letter read: "I am a P'ingtu man. For more than ten years I have known of this doctrine but did not inquire into it. On having an opportunity to inquire, immediately I truly believed. I am deeply in earnest in learning, but there is no pastor here to teach. I earnestly look to the Venerable Board to send out more teachers.... The light of this mercy will shine everywhere, and gratitude will be without limit. I am looking for it as if, when the earth is dry, rain is longed for."

Lottie herself began a desperate letter-writing campaign to the Foreign Mission Board, coining the slogan "Thirty Seed-sowers for North China" in the process.

Eventually Lottie received the news she had been waiting so long to hear. The Woman's Missionary Union had taken up the challenge of organizing a Christmas offering. With tears in her eyes, Lottie read how Annie Armstrong, the newly elected president of the union, had handwritten one thousand letters to various Baptist women's groups to plead for a serious consideration of the project. Annie also had sent out thirty thousand offering envelopes along with three thousand circulars outlining Lottie's work in China. The Woman's Missionary Union had set a goal of raising $2,000 to be used to send missionaries to China. When the money was counted, there was $3,315.26! As a result, three people—Fannie Knight and George Bostick and his wife—had been appointed and were already on their way to China. Laura Barton and Mary Thornton would be not too far behind them.

Lottie was overjoyed. At last more help was finally on the way. She eagerly awaited the arrival of the new missionaries.

Chapter 12

Persecution

It was July 1889, and Lottie was waiting anxiously in Tengchow for the arrival of her new assistant. Finally, one hot afternoon, a shentze pulled into the courtyard of the Little Crossroads, and Fannie Knight, a native of North Carolina, climbed out.

Lottie could only imagine what Fannie must be thinking as she viewed her new surroundings. China was still a dangerous mission field, and Lottie prayed that Fannie would be the kind of helper who could remain brave and joyful even while enduring difficult conditions. Soon the two of them would be headed for P'ingtu, where there was a steadily growing group of Christian converts. Lottie was convinced that eventually there would be a backlash against this group, and she and

Fannie would most likely find themselves in the middle of it.

Fannie Knight was a slight young woman, though not as short as Lottie, with dark brown hair and a ready smile. Lottie liked her immediately. They stayed together in Tengchow at the Little Crossroads while Lottie helped Fannie to outfit herself in Chinese clothing and learn the basics of the Mandarin language.

Not long after Fannie came, the Bosticks arrived. And soon after them came Laura Barton. Lottie and Martha Crawford set about helping them adjust to the new world that would be their home. After two months, it was decided that Fannie would return to P'ingtu with Lottie, Laura would stay in Tengchow to help Martha, and the Bosticks would go to Hwanghsien to help Cicero Pruitt. When two of Lottie's new converts walked all the way from P'ingtu to inquire about Lottie's health and whereabouts, Lottie knew it was time to go "home" to help her new converts.

With the decision to return to P'ingtu, all thoughts of Lottie's returning to the United States on furlough were put on hold, at least until Fannie had mastered the language and was able to carry on the work.

Together Lottie, Fannie, and the Bosticks traveled from Tengchow to Hwanghsien, where Cicero Pruitt greeted them. After enjoying Cicero's hospitality for two days, Lottie and her new helper set out for P'ingtu.

When they arrived back in P'ingtu they found that six converts, two women and four men from Sha-ling, were ready to be baptized. Lottie sent for Cicero Pruitt, who baptized the new converts in a muddy pool just outside the village. From this beginning, the official Sha-ling Baptist Church was formed.

The two women who were baptized were in particular danger. They were both single and soon to be married. Marriage posed a special problem for Christian women because a new bride was expected to worship her husband's ancestors either at their graves or beside stone tablets with the ancestors' names engraved on them. Of course, a Christian could not worship dead people, and this refusal normally made the husband and his entire family very angry. They took it as the worst sign of disrespect.

For one of the women there was a happy ending to the marriage. The bride explained to her husband that she now believed in the foreign God, and the man and his mother accepted this new circumstance and did not force her into ancestral worship. Lottie spent a lot of time with the woman before the wedding and supplied her with Christian books to share with her husband. The woman continued to be a strong Christian all her life.

The second young bride was not so fortunate. Her mother-in-law taunted her mercilessly, first verbally and then physically. Eventually the mother-in-law became so angry with her daughter-in-law that she killed her. Lottie was saddened but not surprised. She began to prepare the group of new converts for more persecution.

It was not only women who were hated for their new religion. In Sha-ling there was an old man by the name of Li-Qin, who had been attracted to Christianity by the lively singing. After attending several of Lottie's meetings, Li-Qin had become convinced that she was speaking the truth of the heavenly way. He stood up at the meeting and told everyone he wanted to become a Christian. It was then that his troubles began. Even though he was a man, he wanted to learn directly from Lottie, so he came privately to her house to talk. Lottie gave him a New Testament, which he treasured, even though he could not read a word of it. When he brought the New Testament home, his sons were very angry. They tried to take the book from their father, but he would not part with it. They hit him, spat on him, and locked him away in the storage room, but still he sang happily of the God who loved him.

This treatment of Li-Qin went on for several weeks, but whenever he had the opportunity, Li-Qin would escape and find Lottie. She encouraged him to endure persecution, assuring him that God could bring good out of any situation. This was not easy advice for Lottie to give. She was an American citizen, and China had signed treaty rights protecting not only American missionaries but also any Chinese person who became a Christian. The treaty stated that these Chinese

Christians could not be persecuted or harmed for their decision to convert and that they had the right to protection. Lottie could have written a stern letter to the American consul in Chefoo requesting such protection, and indeed she seriously considered doing it. However, in the end she decided it would not be wise. The New Testament told countless stories about Christians who were persecuted for their faith, from John the Baptist, who was beheaded, to Stephen, who was stoned to death. Lottie decided it would be a mistake to call in soldiers from a powerful foreign country to force people into stopping their persecution of Christians. It would only confuse the local people and make them think that Christians used force if they did not get their way. Instead, Lottie encouraged Li-Qin to remain strong and pray for the people who were hurting him.

Soon Li-Qin reported to Lottie that his family was trying a new approach. Since he could not read, they had commissioned the family's Confucianist scholar and Li-Qin's nephew, Li Show-ting, to read the New Testament aloud to him. They were sure that this would show Li-Qin how foolish his new beliefs were and he would soon return to worshiping the family's ancestors.

Li Show-ting set out to mock the teachings of Jesus with great gusto. He could hardly wait to point out all the mistakes and inconsistencies to his old uncle. However, Li Show-ting was in for a surprise. As he read aloud, he was held spellbound by what he read. It made so much sense to him, much more sense than anything he had heard from his Confucianist teacher. When he had finished reading to his uncle, Li Show-ting read on into the night alone.

By the next morning, Li Show-ting was standing in Lottie's house asking her to explain what he had read. Lottie, of course, was delighted, and the more she talked to him, the more delighted she became. She could tell he was a brilliant young man who had been jolted into sincerely searching for the truth. Lottie explained what she could, but she was conscious of the fact that she was talking to a man. When Li Show-ting returned to her house day after day, she called for Cicero Pruitt to come and help her.

Before long, Li Show-ting was convinced he wanted to become a Christian like his uncle. He was baptized and welcomed into the stunned Sha-ling Baptist Church. Although Li-Qin had endured much pain and insult, the entire congregation could see the good that had come from his persecution. They would have been even more stunned if they could have seen into the future. Li Show-ting would go on to become a serious Bible scholar. He would travel all over North China preaching the gospel and baptizing those who believed. In his lifetime he would baptize over ten thousand people.

Over Chinese New Year 1890, more trouble developed for the new Christians of Sha-ling and P'ingtu. New Year was the traditional time for Chinese people to venerate their ancestors. However, as word spread that the Chinese Christians refused to worship their ancestors, many of the local people became angry. Li Show-ting was dragged from his house by his brothers and beaten with bamboo rods. When he was nearly unconscious, he was dragged into the center of the village, partly ripping the scalp from his head in the process. In the chaos that followed, however, he was able to escape and flee to Lottie.

In the meantime, Dan Ho-bang, the man who had originally asked Lottie to come and explain the heavenly way to him, was also in great danger at the hands of his irate relatives. They tied him to a pole by his hands and feet and beat him. They screamed at him and kicked him, telling him to renounce this new faith, but he would not. One of the other Christians at Sha-ling ran to P'ingtu to get Lottie. He arrived breathless and desperate. "Unless you come now," he told her, "they will kill Dan Ho-bang. Maybe they have done it already."

Questions about what to do flooded through Lottie's mind. Should she send for a treaty representative? Should she go to Sha-ling alone? Should she take some of the P'ingtu Christian men with her for protection? After a minute or two of thinking about what to do, Lottie called for a shentze. She had led these people to their newfound faith in Jesus Christ, and now she was ready to die helping to protect them if need be.

"Can the mules go faster?" Lottie yelled to the lead man as she bumped her way over the ten miles that lay between P'ingtu and Sha-ling. Finally, as they approached the outer wall of the village, Lottie could hear the mob yelling and cursing. She took a deep breath, praying that God would give her wisdom.

The mob was as violent and bloodthirsty as the messenger had described, and Lottie fought her way to the center of the crowd. She gasped when she saw Dan Ho-bang kneeling with his head in his hands. Blood streamed down his face as he was being kicked and spat upon. Lottie shoved several men with sticks out of the way and ran to his side.

A gasp rose from the mob, and then the people fell silent. Lottie did not know how long the silence would last, so she began to yell out the speech she had prepared in the shentze on the way there. "If you try to destroy the church here, and the Christians who worship in it, you will have to kill me first. Our Master, Jesus, gave His life for us Christians, and now I am ready to die for Him." Then she turned to Dan Ho-bang. "Do not fear, only believe," she told him. "Our Lord Jesus Christ watches over us, and no matter how we are persecuted, Jesus will overcome it."

One of Dan Ho-bang's nephews yelled back, "Then you will die, foreign devil!" With that he lifted a huge sword over his head and aimed it at Lottie. Then, inexplicably, his hand dropped to his side and the sword clattered onto the cobblestone road. With that, the mob's energy appeared to drain, and slowly the people wandered away.

Lottie lifted Dan Ho-bang to his feet and took him back to his house, where several of the Christian men helped wash and tend his wounds. While they worked, Lottie encouraged them all. "Do not give up! The Bible tells us, 'Blessed are the persecuted.' If you keep your faith, others will follow you."

When Dan Ho-bang was well enough to travel, Lottie took him back to P'ingtu with her, where she could oversee his complete recovery.

Although the persecution of Christians in Sha-ling continued, something had changed. Many of the local people were secretly impressed that a white woman would give her life for an old Chinese man. Did she say that Jesus had already given His life for the Christians? they asked one another quietly. Soon a revival began to break out in Sha-ling as new converts flooded into the little Baptist church, eager to learn more about this new faith in Jesus Christ.

Throughout this time, Lottie continued her barrage of letters home to the Foreign Mission Board begging for more missionaries, especially men who could work in the other villages surrounding P'ingtu. Everywhere Lottie went, the Chinese people besieged her with questions. Ten men came by cart to fetch her and take her to the nearby village of Li T'z Yuen. People there had heard of the heavenly way and wanted Lottie to come and explain it to them.

Thankfully, more help did begin to arrive. First Mary Thornton arrived in the summer of 1890, though her arrival was tempered by the sad news that George Bostick's wife had died. In November, T. J. League and his wife arrived especially to help

Lottie. This was a tremendous relief for Lottie. By now, Fannie Knight had been well trained in teaching the gospel in the surrounding villages; Li Show-ting had become an outstanding preacher; and once he had a grasp of the Mandarin language, T. J. League would be able to take up the role of teaching the men. Being a man, T. J. also had authority to baptize new converts.

With these new workers in place, Lottie felt it was time to return to the United States on furlough. It had been thirteen years since she had last been home, and she eagerly booked passage on the maiden voyage of the *Empress of China* for the journey back across the Pacific Ocean.

Chapter 13

Dark Times

It was a blustery summer day in 1891. Lottie and the Pruitts, who also were returning home on furlough, stood on the deck of the *Empress of China*. As the ship pulled away from the dock in Shanghai, Lottie's mind surged with conflicting emotions. On the one hand, she was pleased to be going home to see Edmonia and Ike, her only surviving sister and brother, and to enjoy the peaceful rest she knew she would find in the hills of Virginia. On the other hand, she had a feeling things were about to go very wrong for the Southern Baptist missionaries in Tengchow. Tarleton Crawford had returned to China some time ago, and he had returned even more critical of the Foreign Mission Board and the way it conducted its affairs than he had been before he left. While back in the United States, he had not received the kind of welcome and invitations to speak that he had anticipated as a veteran missionary. This was because he often spoke out against the mission board in a very critical and harsh way when he was invited to speak.

Nor was Tarleton Crawford popular with the other missionaries in Tengchow. He was domineering and grumpy most of the time, and when he got onto an issue, he pushed and pushed until he forced others to agree with his point of view. The latest issue he was pushing was that the Foreign Mission Board should allow the missionaries to run their own affairs without any "interference" from the home board. In his opinion, the mission board should hand over money to the missionaries but should not give advice or direction to them.

In some ways, Lottie agreed with Tarleton. Few members of the Foreign Mission Board had ever been outside the United States, and most of the members had little idea of what missionary life was like. But what to do about it was where Lottie and Tarleton differed. Rather than try to cut the mission board completely out of the picture, Lottie felt that missionaries should communicate more regularly with the board, explaining the situations they encountered in the field until each board member came to understand and respect the problems the missionaries faced overseas.

Now that Lottie and the Pruitts, who shared her view on the matter, were leaving on furlough, Lottie wondered what would happen to the Baptist mission. Three new missionaries were on their way to Tengchow, and Lottie felt a sense of dread for them. Without someone to balance Tarleton Crawford's strong and sometimes hateful talk about the board, what would they think? Lottie knew that the board had not heard the last of Tarleton Crawford. As far as she was concerned, trouble was brewing in North China.

The voyage home was quiet, which suited Lottie completely. She was exhausted from her work and suffered from constant headaches. After the *Empress of China* berthed in San Francisco, Lottie made her way straight to Scottsville, where Edmonia and Isaac were eagerly awaiting her arrival. Even though Southern Baptist women's groups from across the South clamored to have Lottie come and speak to them, she refused their invitations. She did this, she wrote explaining to the groups, not so much for her own sake but for the sake of the Chinese Christians. Lottie was now fifty-one years old, and she feared that if she didn't give her body complete rest for six months, she might not be fit to return to her work in China.

The little house that Lottie jointly owned with Edmonia turned out to be just the place she needed to rest. Lottie had her own room, with a wondrously comfortable bed piled high with fluffy quilts and made with crisp, sweet-smelling linen sheets. It was pure luxury to climb into bed each night. And when Lottie awoke each morning, she was greeted with the sound of Belle the cow waiting to be milked and the chickens scratching around under her window. Edmonia had re-created a tiny replica of the large plantation the Moon family had once owned. Viewmont lay just a few miles up the road, but it was in a state of disrepair, one of hundreds of antebellum mansions whose owners could not pay for their upkeep. Strangers lived in the place now, but Lottie often walked through the tangled, overgrown grounds reliving the happy and carefree days of her youth.

Finally, after six months of care and attention from Edmonia and two servants, Lottie felt well enough to begin her tour of Southern Baptist women's groups. Her tour coincided with the Baptist church's celebration of the centennial of William Carey's going to India as the first Baptist missionary. The celebration was an important event, and Lottie received numerous invitations from groups who wanted a "real" missionary to address them on what it was like to live among the "heathen."

Lottie accepted as many invitations as she could, traveling from nearby Scottsville Baptist Church all the way down the East Coast of the United States to Atlanta, where she attended the Southern Baptist Convention. She was not allowed to address the assembly, of course, since women were not allowed to speak to men in public groups. However, in private gatherings, around the dining table, and over glasses of lemonade, Lottie spoke about her work in China and the constant need for more workers.

While in Georgia, Lottie took a nostalgic train ride to Cartersville, where she and Anna Safford had started the school for girls. Almost the entire town came to meet Lottie, who spent a great deal of time with her former students, now middle-aged women with children of their own.

Wherever she went, Lottie tried to change the image Americans had of Chinese people. In her early letters home, she herself had often referred to them as heathen, but after living among Chinese people for so long, her attitude had dramatically changed. Lottie now grimaced when she heard the word *heathen* used. It was not a description that fit the intelligent and hardworking men and women she had come to know and love in Tengchow and P'ingtu. Whenever an unwitting person used the word, Lottie would gently correct him or her. "Just think," she would say. "The Chinese were a civilized nation while we Europeans were still skulking in the forests of Northern Europe. Join me in praying that the Chinese will become Christians, but be very careful that you respect this and every other group of non-Christian people."

Throughout her time on furlough, Lottie heard snippets of information about what was happening among the missionaries back in China. At a meeting with Henry Tupper, she learned the truth of what was going on. The news was distressing. The trouble Lottie had predicted in North China had come to pass. Several of the new missionary arrivals had left the umbrella of the Foreign Mission Board and along with Tarleton Crawford had formed the "Gospel Mission." Even though she had seen it coming, Lottie still was shocked by his decision. She kept writing to Fannie Knight in P'ingtu, fearing that she too might fall under Tarleton Crawford's "spell." For now, Fannie, along with Laura Barton and the Searses, who had arrived after Lottie left on furlough, were the only missionaries who remained faithful to the Southern Baptists in North China.

When her year of furlough was up, Lottie was eager to return to China, though only a few of her close colleagues were still working there under the umbrella of the Southern Baptists. The Hartwells had returned to Tengchow, and the Pruitts were back at their post in Hwanghsien.

Soon after Lottie arrived back in China, a meeting of the remaining Southern Baptist missionaries was called. But by the time the meeting was held, Lottie had received some devastating news. Fannie Knight had written to say that she had decided to marry one of the missionaries in Tarleton Crawford's group and was moving with them to the group's new location in Taian-fu. However, Fannie became sick and died immediately following her honeymoon. Lottie could not be consoled at the news. Fannie had been a faithful friend and worker, and Lottie had relied on her to keep the mission going in P'ingtu.

When the meeting was finally held, the question became: How should the eight remaining missionaries—the Hartwells, the Pruitts, the Searses, Laura Barton, and Lottie—position themselves to be as effective as possible? After much discussion, it was decided that Lottie, by far the most experienced missionary among the group, should stay in Tengchow. From there she could help Mrs. Hartwell set up a boarding school for girls and teach the women who came to the church. It was also agreed that Lottie should be free to continue her work visiting surrounding villages and sharing the gospel.

Since Lottie would not be returning to P'ingtu to live, the Pruitts agreed to watch over the work there from Hwanghsein. As well, Lottie was convinced that the Christians there, particularly Li Show-ting, had a strong grasp of the gospel and were dedicated to sharing it with others.

Once the arrangements were made about where the various missionaries would serve, Lottie was ready to settle back into the Little Crossroads. Before she did so, however, she wanted to do one thing. She decided to visit the Christians in P'ingtu and Sha-ling to let them know that she was fine and trusted them to go on alone without her.

The four-day journey by shentze to P'ingtu was just as bumpy as ever. Still, the discomfort was well worth it. And the Christians at Sha-ling were exuberant to see their missionary again. They hastily arranged a baptism service in which eleven new members were added to the rapidly growing church. And that was not all. On property that Lottie had purchased before leaving on furlough, the church members had built a simple Chinese-style church with a school attached to it.

Lottie was pleased by all she saw. She was proud of the way these Chinese Christians were taking ownership of their church and reaching out to others on their own initiative with the gospel. When it was time for Lottie to leave, no one wanted her to go. However, Lottie felt confident that the work would go on without her. As she left the people she had nurtured and encouraged through heartache and persecution, Lottie invited them to visit her anytime they were in Tengchow. Many of them said they would come, and they did.

The Little Crossroads became a hub of hospitality for Christians from all over North China. Christians made their way to Lottie's house to pour out their troubles and seek advice. Paupers and beggars came, too. Lottie always offered them a place to stay and gave them food and a little money if she had any herself.

As the years rolled by, Lottie's workload continued to increase. She set up a school for girls, and then later one for boys. She taught Sunday school and tried to visit two villages each day. All the while, she watched and listened as the political climate in China began to darken. By early 1900, Lottie became convinced that the leader of China, the empress dowager, was deliberately stirring up antiforeign feelings among the Chinese people. Lottie wrote to the U.S. consul, John Fowler, about her suspicions. As she carried on with her work, Lottie had the uneasy sense that China was about to explode with anti-Western hatred.

One winter morning, a loud thumping at the door awoke Lottie. When Lottie opened the door, there stood a young Christian man from Laichow, a town halfway between Hwanghsien and P'ingtu. "You must come. There is terrible trouble, and the Christians are asking for you!" he said as he hurried into the warm house.

Soon Lottie was serving the young man lomein noodles and asking what he meant.

"It's Wai-Sung, the magistrate at Laichow," said the young man, warming his hands around the bowl of noodles. "He has never liked the Christians, but now there are so many rumors circulating about the evil things Christians do that he decided to punish us."

"What has he done?" Lottie asked, dreading to hear the answer.

"Three days ago he arrested thirteen Christians on robbery charges. Of course, it is all a lie, and he knows it." The young man gulped some noodles before continuing. "The soldiers tied the men's queues (pigtails) onto their horses' saddles and dragged the men all the way from Laichow to Laichowfu."

"Did they die?" Lottie asked in a whisper.

"No," replied her young visitor. "Pastor Li Show-ting heard what was going on, and he demanded the magistrate stop the horses. When I left to come here, the Christians were all in the prison at P'ingtu. You must come and help us. Everyone is asking for you, even Pastor Li."

Lottie took a deep breath and closed her eyes. What should she do? The roads outside Tengchow had become dangerous to travel in the past few months. Mobs of Boxers, men who were sworn haters of all foreigners, roamed the area. They reveled in destroying anything foreign, including churches and books, but worse, they enjoying hunting down and killing Christians, whether Chinese or foreign. In going to the aid of the Christians in P'ingtu, Lottie would be risking her life. Yet it was unthinkable for her not to go.

Eventually Lottie came up with a plan. It was dangerous, but it might work. "I need to hire a shentze like the ones the city officials use," she told the young man. "Do you think you could get me one?"

"I will try," he replied and immediately prepared to go in search of one.

While he was gone, Lottie borrowed some clothing from a local official she knew. She put on the long robe with its dangling cuffs and then the short red jacket all officials wore. She smoothed her hair back, not in the usual bun on top of her head but into a single pigtail at the back. Then she placed a skullcap with a large red button on it on top of her head. Lottie looked at herself in the oval mirror on the wall, hoping that she would be able to pass herself off as an official traveling on business to P'ingtu.

Soon the young man came back with a genuine official's shentze, complete with heavy curtains.

Lottie gathered some food for the journey and climbed into the shentze. She opened the front flap and folded her arms across the bar, just as she had seen many officials do. "Let's go with God's help," she said to the young man, who then ordered the mule drivers to begin the journey.

For four days, Lottie sat in the shentze keeping up her official pose, staring proudly down at the crowds that greeted her. She saw several mobs of Boxers, but when they saw the official shentze they scattered.

Finally Lottie's caravan made its way into P'ingtu. Good news awaited. The thirteen Christians were all alive, and Pastor Li Show-ting had managed to get them released from prison. However, all of the men were injured, some from being dragged along behind the horses, others from the various forms of torture used by the prison wardens. Lottie comforted and encouraged the men as best she could with her words, but the fact that she had risked her life to come to their aid was the greatest encouragement of all.

It wasn't long before Lottie realized that her presence in P'ingtu was putting the Christians there in danger. Boxer informants were in every corner of the town, and anyone who was seen with or around Lottie was immediately singled out as a target for the Boxers to strike at. As much as she hated to admit it, Lottie knew that the Chinese Christians would have a better chance of surviving this persecution if she was not around.

Reluctantly she made her way back through Hwanghsien to Tengchow, where terrible news awaited her. The Boxer uprising had turned bloody. Tales of terror began circulating. In Hebei province, sixteen missionaries had been stoned and then beheaded on June 28, 1900. In Heilongjiang province, a blind Chinese preacher had been beheaded in a temple, along with more than three hundred of his converts.

Even though she had anticipated that bad times were ahead, Lottie was appalled at the loss of life. The Boxers were killing some of the brightest, best-educated, and most honest people in the country.

On July 1, Lottie was hosting a wedding in her home when news of the decree arrived. American consul John Fowler had ordered all foreigners to evacuate the province. Lottie had no problem complying with his order. She knew it was getting extremely dangerous, and just as in P'ingtu, her presence in Tengchow was beginning to place her Chinese friends in jeopardy. Quickly she threw a few clothes and some books into her trunk, locked the door of the Little Crossroads, and headed for Tengchow's harbor. Waiting at the dock for the missionaries was the *Hai-Chi,* a gunboat captained by Mr. Sah, a devout Christian who considered it an honor to risk his life to get the missionaries to the relative safety of Chefoo.

As the *Hai-Chi* steamed out into the harbor, Lottie looked with dismay around her. On the shore she could see Boxers swarming everywhere, waving sticks and guns and yelling threats. On the horizon, Russian gunboats lay at anchor, waiting for their next victim. (The Russians were using the Boxer Rebellion as an opportunity to try to exert more control over North China.) Mr. Sah skillfully guided the *Hai-Chi* past the gunboats and rendezvoused with the U.S.S. *Yorktown.* The fleeing missionaries transferred to the *Yorktown* and were ferried to Chefoo.

Chapter 14

A Growing Mission

Lottie was glad to disembark the *Yorktown* and get her feet back on dry land. Chefoo was overflowing with displaced foreigners and was awash in rumors about what was happening inland away from the safety of the treaty ports. Lottie's heart grew heavy as the number of casualties of the Boxer Rebellion grew. On July 9, 1900, George Farthing, an English Baptist missionary, and his wife and three children were beheaded in Shanxi province. Soon forty-six more foreigners had been killed there.

As the grim statistics began to roll in, Lottie realized that it was going to be a while before she or any other missionary would be allowed to leave a treaty port and venture inland again. As she wondered about what she should do, Lottie found her thoughts drifting toward Japan. She decided to relocate to Fukuoka, Japan, and await the end of the Boxer Rebellion. After catching the first available steamer out of Chefoo, Lottie changed ships in Shanghai and was soon steaming her way across the Yellow Sea to Japan. By mid-July 1900, she was a guest of the McCollums, Southern Baptist missionaries in Fukuoka.

In characteristic fashion, Lottie set straight to work. She could not hope to learn enough Japanese to be useful in evangelistic work right away, so she took a job teaching English at a commercial school. There was no set textbook for the class; each teacher chose his or her own reading material. Of course, Lottie chose the Bible. Within a few weeks, her brightest students were able to read passages of it to her. After they had read a passage, she explained its meaning to them as best she could. It wasn't too long before three of the young men in Lottie's class had become Christians.

No matter how involved she became spreading the gospel in Japan, Lottie longed to hear news of China and her Christian friends in Tengchow and the surrounding areas.

Finally, after nearly a year, the Boxer Rebellion came to an end when eight nations formed a joint army, invaded Peking, overthrew the empress dowager, and forced the Chinese government to sign a surrender agreement. However, the final toll of the rebellion was high. Over 32,000 Chinese Christians were slaughtered, along with 230 foreign missionary men, women, and children.

In April 1901, things were finally calm enough for Lottie to head back to Tengchow and the Little Crossroads. Most Christians in Tengchow had survived unscathed, and the church was still intact. However, life was not quite so favorable for those Christians in P'ingtu and Sha-ling, where many deaths and beatings and house burnings had taken place.

As part of the surrender agreement with foreign powers, the Chinese government had promised to repay those people whose property was destroyed or damaged by the rampaging Boxers. The Baptist churches in Shantung province asked for only what was a fair price to cover their losses, and not a penny more. This basic honesty and the way in which Christians had endured persecution and even death greatly impressed the local people.

When Lottie returned to Tengchow, she found more doors open to her than ever before. The local people wanted to know what power was so strong that it would cause a Christian to die with dignity and hope. Within a few months, there were over a hundred baptisms of new converts.

The Boxer Rebellion had hit the world headlines, too, and renewed the interest of American Christians in reaching China with the gospel. Once the doors of China were opened to foreigners again, new missionaries began to flood into the country. Lottie was particularly pleased to welcome those who had been called to missionary service as a result of her influence and example. It was the fulfillment of a dream.

Jessie Pettigrew, the first registered nurse ever appointed by the Foreign Mission Board, arrived in Tengchow. She had been raised on stories of Lottie Moon's heroism and sacrifice. Mary Willeford came, too. As a small girl in Sunday school, she had been inspired by stories of Lottie's adventures. A doctor, Thomas Ayers, and his family also arrived. Dr. Ayers had asked to be stationed in Hwangshien because he had been moved by the story of the Pruitts, who served there.

Now, at the close of 1901, Shantung province had two medical missionaries, a nurse and a doctor. The next step as far as Lottie was concerned was a hospital for them to work in. Lottie and Dr. Ayers wrote to the Foreign Mission Board asking for seven thousand dollars. If the money was granted, it would fund the board's first venture into building a hospital.

Lottie had been so busy with her work that she hardly noticed that as 1902 rolled around, it had been nine and a half years since her last furlough. Mainly as a result of Lottie's influence, the Foreign Mission Board had begun a policy whereby missionaries were to come home on furlough every ten years whether they needed a break or not. Lottie was reluctant to leave her Chinese friends, but she saw the trip as an opportunity to stir up interest in the proposed hospital and raise money for it.

In the summer of 1902, Lottie traveled to Chefoo to have suitable Western clothes made for her. She had been wearing Chinese-style clothing for so long that she had little idea of American fashions. The clothing she ordered from the dressmaker—long, black high-necked dresses and silk bonnets—was hopelessly out of date, but somehow it fit Lottie's image. Lottie returned to the United States in January 1903, a quaint stranger in a world that had once been her home.

This time, Lottie did not have a house to return to. Two years earlier, Edmonia had sold Bonheur, the house the two sisters had owned, and begun a life of wandering about the South in search of a climate that would bring relief to her various medical ailments. Lottie went to stay with her brother Isaac, who now lived in Crewe, Virginia. The folks at the Baptist church at Crewe were delighted to have such a legendary person as Lottie staying among them.

From Crewe, Lottie fanned out across the countryside to speak to women's groups and visit old friends and family members. She visited Mamie, her only niece, who was married and living in Norfolk, Virginia. She also saw her sister Orianna's sons and their families. Most of them now lived in and around Roanoke, Virginia. While Lottie was in Roanoke, Edmonia came to visit her. It was a sad reunion for Lottie, who was shocked at how old and worn her sister looked, despite the fact that Edmonia was ten years younger than Lottie. Eddie acted as if all the good times in life were behind her and only gloom and loneliness lay ahead. Lottie grew concerned over Edmonia's mental state and hoped that her sister would soon settle down somewhere rather than live in one boardinghouse after another, as she presently did.

Everywhere Lottie went, people pleaded with her not to go back to China. Lottie was now sixty-two years old, and it was obvious that the years of hard pioneering work had taken their toll on her body. However, Lottie would not consider staying in the United States. America was simply not her home anymore; her heart was in China.

While Lottie was in America, a professor arranged for her to attend the University of Virginia commencement ceremonies in the summer of 1903. He also organized for her to go to two formal dinners where President Theodore Roosevelt was the guest speaker. One of the dinners was held at Monticello, the neighboring estate to Viewmont, which Lottie's uncle had once owned. As Lottie sat down to an eight-course meal, memories of growing up in and around Viewmont and Monticello flooded her thoughts. It all seemed so far away and so different from the life she now led in China. Monticello was a magnificent home, but in Lottie's mind it did not compare to the Little Crossroads in Tengchow, where Lottie felt at home now. That was where she belonged, sharing the gospel with those who had not yet heard it.

As her year of furlough progressed, Lottie grew dismayed to see how little the Southern Baptists were doing to help the poor black people of the South. Whenever she had the opportunity, Lottie would visit them, bringing food and clothing for the children.

Finally, on February 27, 1904, after thirteen months in the United States, Lottie headed for "home." She boarded the steamship *China* in San Francisco. As the harbor faded from view, Lottie thought about the three other times she had left America. On those occasions, she had not known whether she would see friends and family again. This time, she knew for sure that she would never again see some of the people closest to her. Her brother Isaac was in poor health and was not expected to live long, and Edmonia's condition was deteriorating. Edmonia seemed to have lost the will to go on living. Lottie had heard that this had happened to a lot of southerners who'd had their land and lifestyle ripped away from them in the Civil War. All the family traditions and connections were gone, and Eddie did not appear to have the ability to build new ones.

Many changes had taken place in Shantung province while Lottie was away. One change, which particularly pleased her, was that the citizens of Sha-ling had decided to empty their ancient temple and use the building as a public school. Lottie could not think of a better example of what Christianity could do for a country. These people wanted to leave behind their superstitions and concentrate on the welfare and education of their children.

The missionaries had made numerous changes among themselves as well. Cicero Pruitt had opened a theological school. The school was for men, of course, but plans were in the works for a women-church-workers training school to be run by Mary Willeford, a new missionary. Jesse Owen, another new missionary, was having a great deal of success with evangelism in the countryside, and he, too, had opened a school.

Best of all, in Hwanghsien, the hospital that Lottie and Dr. Ayers had dreamed about was finally under way. The First Baptist Church of Macon, Georgia, had provided most of the money for it to be built.

In addition to everything else going on, the Chinese Christians were organizing themselves into groups to address such issues as unbinding women's feet, evangelism, and running Sunday schools. Lottie was pleased with all the progress that had occurred while she was away, and she began to think about where she could be the most useful.

In the end, Lottie decided that her place was back in education, and she returned to what she had done in the very beginning, setting up and administrating schools. It seemed that after the Boxer Rebellion, everyone wanted to go to school. Lottie remembered the first girls school she had started in Tengchow thirty years before. Then, she'd had to beg for girls to be allowed to attend class. And even then, she was able to attract only those girls who were considered society's castoffs. Now grown men showed up at school asking how their children could be admitted, and women from the highest families in town sent letters to Lottie requesting that places be set aside for their daughters. To cope with the demand, Lottie purchased more land on North Street to expand the existing school there, which came to be known as Memorial School. She also opened a grade school for small children and encouraged the setting up of a girls school in P'ingtu.

Lottie did not get out into the villages in the countryside as much as she had when she was younger. However, many people from the villages found their way to her house in Tengchow. As many as fifteen women and children at a time would stay with her. They came for medical help, for Christian instruction, or merely because they had heard that the old American woman would give them food and a warm place to sleep. Lottie was delighted to help these women in any way she could. She read the Bible to them and taught them hymns. She even taught many of them to read and then gave them a Bible to take home with them. Of course, hosting these people in her home took a lot of money; the cook had to be paid, food had to be purchased, and fresh matting and coal had to be provided for the k'ang. Despite the cost to her, Lottie accepted everyone who wanted to visit her.

In the years following the Boxer Rebellion, the Chinese government went through a period of great upheaval. As a result, one of the things that changed was the old civil service examination that every person who wanted to hold office had to pass. Tengchow had always been one of the cities where these examinations were held, and much of the commerce and money flowing into town came as a result of the students who poured in to prepare for and take the exams. When the civil service exams were abolished, Tengchow lost its place of importance. Many people moved away, and it was decided that the mission's theological school would relocate to Hwanghsien, close to the new hospital. Most of the Southern Baptist missionaries in Tengchow moved with the school, but not Lottie. There was still work to be done in Tengchow, and the Little Crossroads was a home away from home for hundreds of Chinese Christians. Lottie simply could not move.

Thankfully, about the time everyone else left, two new recruits arrived from the United States: Ella Jeter and Ida Taylor, neither of whom understood a word of Chinese. However, they were eager to learn and serve alongside Lottie in any way they could. By the end of 1906, both Ella and Ida had adapted remarkably well to life in China and were ready to take charge of the girls school, which now had over fifty students.

The following year, Lottie received a letter from her old friend Martha Crawford. The pair had continued to write to each other even through the most difficult of times when Martha's husband, Tarleton, had left the covering of the Southern Baptists over the policies of the Foreign Mission Board. Now Tarleton was dead, and Martha was free to visit

Lottie. When the seventy-seven-year-old missionary arrived in Tengchow, she was as energetic as ever, and soon she and Lottie were holding meetings together around the town.

Martha had a special request for Lottie. When her husband had died, many of the missionaries who had followed him when he split from the Southern Baptists began to question why they had left. They started to realize that a lot of the drive to separate had been based on Tarleton's bitter talk, and they wanted to set things right with the Foreign Mission Board and come back under the umbrella of the Southern Baptists. Since Lottie was the one missionary who had been able to remain friends with both sides of the dispute, Martha asked her to try to smooth the way for the wayward missionaries to return. Lottie was delighted to do so; she hated to see missionaries fighting among themselves. She wrote a letter to Robert Willingham, the new secretary of the Foreign Mission Board, raising the issue of the missionaries who had followed Tarleton Crawford. As a result, almost all of these missionaries returned to work under the auspices of the Southern Baptists in China.

As delighted as Lottie was at seeing her old friend Martha again, she was even more delighted when news reached her that Robert Willingham would be coming to China to see firsthand the work of the missionaries there. This was the first time ever that a secretary of the Foreign Mission Board was going to see for himself what it was like to be a missionary in China. Lottie believed that if Robert Willingham saw the opportunities that existed for spreading the gospel, he would go home and stir up American congregations to become more involved.

Robert Willingham experienced even more of the missionary life than he had intended. Just as he arrived, there was an outbreak of meningitis in Tengchow, followed swiftly by bubonic plague. After his visit, he went home with a fresh appreciation of the conditions under which Lottie and the other missionaries in China lived. But, of course, by now such conditions seemed normal to Lottie, who had been a missionary in China for thirty-four years.

Chapter 15

Do You Smell Smoke?

Robert Willingham returned home and stirred up American congregations. During the following year, 1908, more missionary recruits came to join the work in China. Much to her delight, Lottie discovered she was the inspiration for many of these new missionaries who had decided to come to China. Dr. James Gaston and his wife were the first of the new recruits to arrive. James Gaston had not even been a Southern Baptist when he first heard about Lottie Moon and her work in China. He had been so impressed with what she was doing that he had joined the Southern Baptist church and began to pray regularly for Lottie. That had been ten years before, and now he was in Tengchow ready to learn Mandarin and all about Chinese culture from the veteran missionary herself.

By now Lottie knew exactly how to ease a new missionary into the culture. She had outfitted one of the rooms at the Little Crossroads as a Western-style guest room, complete with wrought-iron bed and side tables. Lottie did not need these home comforts herself, but she knew from her own and Edmonia's experience thirty-five years before that a missionary needed to be gently guided into the pattern of life in China to reduce the effects of culture shock. As soon as Lottie felt that the Gastons had adjusted to their new environment, she sent them to Laichowfu, where they were assigned to open another Baptist hospital.

Soon after the Gastons left, another missionary, Wayne Adams, took up residence in Lottie's guest room. Wayne was fresh out of seminary, where he had heard numerous stories—and a few tall tales—about Lottie Moon. He had turned down a comfortable pastorate in America to come to China. Wayne also had a fiancée, Floy White, who was finishing her studies in the United States before joining him in China. Lottie decided that Wayne would make a fine missionary and set about teaching him.

A few weeks after his arrival, Wayne was sitting and talking with Lottie over dinner. Very few Chinese people knew much about the rest of the world. Indeed, many Chinese scholars still believed the earth was flat. As a result, Lottie enjoyed having an American guest to discuss world events with. As they talked, Wayne suddenly jumped out of his chair. "Do you smell smoke?" he asked.

Lottie put her nose in the air. Because there was rarely a chimney in a Chinese home, there was always the faint, lingering smell of smoke around. But this time it was different. "I believe I do," Lottie said, thinking quickly. "Check outside, Wayne, and I'll look in the kitchen."

Lottie had only reached the doorway when she heard Wayne yelling. "It's the house next door! Get out!"

Lifting the hem of her skirt so as not to trip on it, Lottie rushed from the house. Wayne was right. Huge flames were shooting out of the empty house next door.

Other neighbors quickly began to gather, not to help but to curse. "See, the old devil woman's house is going to burn down," one woman crooned to her toddler. "The gods have had enough of her evil ways."

"Finally you are getting what you have deserved!" spat another hostile neighbor.

Lottie tried not to take what they were saying to heart, though after living among these people for so long, their continued antagonism still surprised and troubled her. Now was not the time to dwell on that, however; she had to concentrate on saving her house.

"Quickly, Wayne, get the bucket from the back porch and fetch water. Perhaps it's not too late to stop the flames from reaching my roof," Lottie yelled.

Wayne ran to get the bucket and then ran to the well. Lottie watched in dismay as the swelling crowd hardly made way for him to get through. "God," she prayed silently, "bring us help, or my house will be destroyed."

As she finished her prayer, she heard a yell from down the street. Lottie watched as a contingent of the mandarin's soldiers came running into view. They carried buckets, and as soon as they reached the Little Crossroads, they formed a human chain to pass the water from the well to the house, where several of them threw the water at the roof.

Soon some of the local Christians joined in, and much to Lottie's relief, the danger passed. The wind also shifted a little, helping to keep the flames off her house. However, the wind shift now put the house on the other side in danger of burning. The family that lived there rushed around, yelling and begging for help.

"We must help them," Wayne told the exhausted Christians.

"Yes, we must," said one of the Christian men as the group manned their buckets again.

A murmur went through the crowd when they saw what was happening. They began to whisper to one another, wondering why these Christians were prepared to help people who despised them.

"Climb that ladder," Lottie directed one of the men in the crowd, "and Ling will hand you a bucket. Throw the water as far into the flames as you can."

Soon many of the neighbors had been pressed into service. Christians and non-Christians worked side by side until the fire was out.

When she finally lay down on her k'ang that night, Lottie was exhausted. She could still smell the smoke, and one of the Christian men had offered to stay up all night to make sure the fire did not rekindle. But Lottie was proud, too. Proud that the Christians had accepted the challenge to bless people who often cursed them. She hoped it would lead to a new openness among the people of Tengchow to the gospel.

Despite Lottie's obvious joy at the influx of new missionaries, two matters weighed heavily on her heart. The first was the death of her sister Edmonia. Eddie had moved to Stark, Florida, where she lived a reclusive life in a tiny clapboard house. She had died a lonely and sad death, and Lottie wished she could have been able to be there at the end to cheer up her little sister. The two of them had been through so much together, pioneering the way for single women missionaries to work in China. Indeed, Lottie doubted she would have even become a missionary if Edmonia had not paved the way for her.

As Lottie looked around at the progress Christianity had made during the thirty-five years since she and Edmonia had worked together in Tengchow, she knew her sister would have been proud. The Southern Baptists now oversaw sixteen churches in North China, along with fifty-six schools teaching over one thousand students. There were forty-two Chinese male evangelists and fourteen female, and over two thousand Christians were baptized church members.

The second matter that weighed heavy on Lottie was the thirty-two thousand dollars the Foreign Mission Board was in debt. The debt had arisen because of the way the board raised the money to meet its budget. At conventions and conferences, missionaries and speakers would get up and stir the listeners with the need for more missionaries and funds to maintain the denomination's mission projects around the world. The participants at these gatherings were mostly pastors, who were asked to pledge as much money as possible to missions on behalf of their churches. Of course, they usually pledged a lot of money, thinking they could pass on the vision for missions to their congregations, who would in turn donate the pledged amount. However, this was not always the case. Many pastors' enthusiasm for missions fizzled in light of new church building projects and Sunday school budgets. As a result, the churches were not able to meet their pledges. In the meantime, the Foreign Mission Board went ahead and sent out new missionaries and authorized new projects based upon the assumption that the total amount of money pledged would come in. It never did, and the board was in constant financial crisis, especially around April, when the financial accounts for the year were tallied.

When Lottie read about the debt, which represented the difference between what was pledged and what had been collected, she was saddened. If only people in the United States could see the changed lives and the new hope the missionaries had brought to people in China, Lottie was certain they would eagerly meet their pledges. Lottie felt she had to do what little she could to help the financial situation, so she asked that the small inheritance she received from Edmonia's estate be sent directly to the Foreign Mission Board for debt reduction.

Despite the financial crisis, three more missionaries were sent to China. One of them was Wayne Adams's fiancée, Floy White. Lottie was torn. She welcomed the new missionaries with open arms, but she feared there would not be enough money in the budget to keep them all.

With Floy's arrival, a wedding date was soon set. The wedding was a mixture of Chinese and Western traditions, which Lottie herself organized in great detail. Lottie had become very fond of Wayne during the time he had stayed with her and wanted to give him the best wedding possible. Along with some helpers, Lottie decorated Wayne and Floy's new house in red, the color of celebration in China. Missionaries came from all over North China to the wedding, and Lottie arranged a delicious wedding feast of roast goose, soup, boiled fish, salad, vegetables, dessert, even candies for them all. After the wedding reception, the couple left in a new sedan chair that Wayne had purchased for his bride.

In 1910, just a few months after the wedding, all the Southern Baptist missionaries and Chinese workers serving in Shantung province met together in Chefoo. Lottie was thrilled to see old friends again, especially those missionaries who had followed

Tarleton Crawford but had now chosen to come back under the covering of the Foreign Mission Board. Lottie and some of the older missionaries reminisced about their early days in Shantung province when there were few Chinese converts. Now there were thousands of Christians. Some of the evangelists and teachers attending the gathering were children, even grandchildren, of some of the earliest converts.

One of the women missionaries serving in P'ingtu related a story to Lottie. She had been out visiting a remote village when she came across a very old woman who was singing hymns and reciting passages of Scripture. When the missionary asked the woman where she had learned them, the old woman replied that a missionary had visited twenty years before and given her a Bible and taught her the hymns. The woman had waited patiently for twenty years for another Christian worker to come so that she could be baptized. This and other stories like it touched Lottie deeply. They highlighted some of the successes the missionaries had had over the years, but they also drew attention to the work that still needed to be done. There were still many people who had never heard the gospel, and many more workers were needed.

Another need was growing in China. The crops had failed in Central China, starting a famine that soon began to affect the coastal regions as well. Lottie wrote to everyone she could think of, pleading for money to buy food and clothing for the victims of the famine. She could not get used to seeing people lying in the streets dying from hunger. As a result, she took in as many needy people as she could, and her old cook was constantly boiling millet to feed the crowd that gathered around the Little Crossroads.

A plague hit soon after the famine, killing even more people and generally unsettling the local population. The thoughts of some people began to turn toward political change. By 1911 most Chinese people had some idea of how foreign countries worked, and they wanted a republic like the United States to replace their ailing Manchu dynasty. Privately, Lottie also hoped for change. She did not see how the old government could adapt fast enough to the changing times, but she never made her views public. As a foreigner, Lottie was careful about what she said. If change came, she knew it would have to come from the Chinese people themselves, and any hint that the missionaries were involved would place every Christian's life in jeopardy. Instead, she waited quietly to see what would happen in the country.

Chapter 16

Christmas Eve

Lottie was standing outside her back door when Zhang, one of her schoolboys, ran around the side of the house. "Look," he said, turning his head proudly for her to see.

Lottie gasped. The boy's queue (pigtail) was gone, chopped off at shoulder length. "What have you done, Zhang?" she asked, even though the answer was obvious.

"I chopped it off," he replied. "Aren't you pleased with me?"

Taking a deep breath, Lottie drew herself up to her full four feet ten inches. "Go home quickly and reattach it before you come back!" she said, knowing that cutting off his queue in sympathy with the rebels trying to overthrow the Manchu government could put the boy and his family in danger.

Zhang gave Lottie a hurt look and hurried off the way he had come. When he was out of sight, Lottie sat down in her rocking chair, put her head in her hands, and wept for China. She read the newspapers and took a keen interest in politics and was quite sure she knew what lay ahead for her adopted land. A revolution was under way in the country. A rebel force loyal to Sun Yat-sen, who advocated the establishment of a Chinese republic and a democratic form of government, had engaged the forces of the Manchu dynasty in battle. While the rebels seemed to be making headway in their quest, the fighting was often ferocious, as the imperial forces refused to give up the fight. As a result, the death toll, especially among innocent civilians, was high.

Lottie prayed that Christians in Shantung province would remain strong and would behave in a manner honoring to God during the struggle. Regrettably, some of them did not grasp the full meaning of Christianity, as Lottie found out.

One day, soon after Zhang had visited to show Lottie his chopped-off queue, several other young Christian men came to see her. "Miss Moon, we have been able to defeat the pagan god in the city temple!" they exclaimed joyfully.

"What do you mean?" Lottie asked Huang, the oldest of the group.

Huang stepped forward. "We met the revolutionaries on their way to smash down the idols at the temple, and we decided to join them. We thought about all the times people from the temple have persecuted us, and it seemed like such a good opportunity to rid the city of such evil forever."

"So what exactly did you do?" Lottie inquired, not sure she wanted to know.

"We entered the temple. You should have seen everyone scatter when they saw the guns," Huang grinned. "Then we took all the idols down. The soldiers smashed some of them, and so did we. Then we took the rest to my home. What should we do with them?"

Lottie could feel herself ready to explode. "What should you do with them? You should march them right back to where you got them and beg the forgiveness of those poor people," she announced forcefully.

"I don't understand," Huang replied. "Didn't you want the idols taken down?"

"Sit down," Lottie said, pointing to the bench on the veranda. "You must think before you act in these times. Today the revolutionaries looted the pagan temple, stealing their sacred objects and harassing the worshipers. That is religious persecution, the very thing we Christians object to. What would you say if they came into our church and did the same thing? Our Lord teaches us to do unto others as we would have them do unto us, not to avenge ourselves and attack those we disagree with. Such behavior is not Christian!"

Everyone in the group hung his head. "What should we do?" asked one of them.

"You must return everything you have stolen and apologize," Lottie replied, more gently this time. She could see the young Christians were genuinely remorseful.

The young men followed through on Lottie's advice, and everywhere she went, Lottie made a point of apologizing for the Christians' behavior, saying that religious persecution was not the Christian way of doing things.

These were not the only incidents that upset Lottie in the fall of 1911. Everyone, it seemed, was stockpiling weapons, waiting for some big and perhaps final showdown. The military came to the Little Crossroads bringing guns to offer Lottie. "The time is coming when you will be needing these," they told her.

Lottie, however, just hid her head in her hands. She could not imagine any circumstance that would induce her to fire a gun at a Chinese person, friend or enemy. "Take them away," she ordered, thinking back to the time thirty-eight years before when, after hearing how Tarleton Crawford had threatened an angry crowd of Chinese men with a gun, she had vowed never to do such a thing herself.

The military had been correct, though. Within weeks, Southern Baptist missions throughout the region were under attack. The U.S. consul put out a call for all foreigners to evacuate the area. Lottie's missionary colleagues in P'ingtu and at the hospital in Hwanghsien flooded into Tengchow. Lottie's heart broke at the news. How were the Chinese

Christian workers in Hwanghsien going to carry on at the hospital without help? She could not bear to think of her Chinese friends battling on alone. Somehow, she decided, she had to get to them.

Without telling her fellow missionaries, Lottie made her way to Hwanghsien. She was the only foreigner going into the war zone, as everyone else was fleeing. When she arrived at the hospital, a number of the workers wept openly. At seventy-one, Lottie had risked her life to stand with them in crisis.

For ten days Lottie lived and worked at the hospital. Casualties from both sides of the conflict were treated. Dr. Ayers and the other missionaries, hearing of what Lottie had done, became so worried about her and the hospital that they risked their own lives to return. When they reached Hwanghsien, they found Lottie calmly dispensing cups of tea and comforting the patients.

Once the missionary staff had returned to the hospital, Lottie felt free to return to Tengchow and the Little Crossroads. The only trouble was that conditions on the road back were worse than ever, with the rebels and imperial soldiers facing off against each other just a few miles from town. Despite this danger, Lottie could not be dissuaded from making the trip. It was time for her to go home, and that was what she was going to do.

When the Christians in Hwanghsien realized that Lottie could not be stopped, they sent word to the commanding generals on both sides, informing them that Lottie Moon, the old woman missionary from Tengchow, would be passing through the battle zone in a shentze at 10 A.M.

Dr. Ayers also insisted that a young missionary, Carey Daniel, go with Lottie, even though she did not think it was necessary. Lottie had an unwavering faith that she would make it through the firing line unscathed. And she was right. As 10 A.M. approached, Lottie's convoy was on its way. Lottie sat tall and proud as she passed between the two armies. Not a single shot was fired, though as soon as her shentze was clear of the area, Lottie could hear the gunfire start up again.

Lottie hurried home to tend to the women and children who had taken refuge in the rooms attached to her house. No matter how stretched her finances were, she always took in anyone who asked and shared whatever she was eating with them.

Conditions in Tengchow continued to worsen. So many people from outlying villages had flooded into the city, thinking it would be safer there, that little food was available, at any price. Despite the food crisis, Lottie battled on.

One old beggar woman had been so hungry she threw herself from a bridge outside town in an attempt to end her life. Instead of falling into the water and drowning, the woman landed on some rocks. As people crossed the bridge, they stopped and looked down at the woman, who now lay motionless below, her life slowly ebbing away.

As soon as Lottie heard of the old woman's plight, she rushed to the bridge and paid some onlookers to carry the woman to the guest room at the Little Crossroads. Lottie dressed her wounds and gave her food and water. The woman lived in Lottie's care and comfort for several weeks before she finally died from internal injuries. A number of Christians in Tengchow questioned why Lottie would "waste" time on an old, dying beggar woman. To Lottie the answer was simple: Every life was equally precious to God, and Lottie had come to China to serve anyone He placed in her path.

Lottie had the sorrowful task of watching another person die. Jesse Broadman Hartwell, who had first come to China as a missionary in 1857 and had spent thirty-five of the past fifty-five years serving in China, was suffering from a fatal illness. The Chinese Christians were distraught to see their old teacher dying, but everyone took comfort in the unusual event that accompanied his death. In the hours before his death, J. B. Hartwell seemed to go into a deep coma. From within the coma he would call out to local Christians who had already died, as if he were seeing them in the distance. Everyone around him, including Lottie, was heartened by what they saw. Surely, they told each other, Pastor Hartwell is catching a glimpse of heaven. This idea was dismissed, however, when he called out the name of a local deacon who had recently gone to South China as a missionary. Since everyone knew the deacon was still alive, they decided that J. B. Hartwell's talk reflected the hallucinations of a dying man.

Jesse Broadman Hartwell eventually died. At his funeral was a man who had just traveled up from South China and had some news for the gathering. The man whom J. B. Hartwell had greeted in his comalike state had died unexpectedly several days before, right about the time his name had been called out by the old missionary. Word of this spread quickly throughout Tengchow, and many people wanted Lottie to tell them more about heaven and the Christian God.

By May 1912, the revolution was over. The forces and ideas of Sun Yat-sen had prevailed. Two hundred sixty-seven years of Manchu rule over China came to an end, and a new Chinese republic was declared. Lottie was secretly delighted by the outcome of the revolution, although drought and famine lingered on. As a result, Lottie wrote many letters to the Foreign Mission Board trying to press on the members the enormity of people's struggle to survive in China. The board members were overwhelmed by problems of their own, however. That year, the board's missions budget fell short by fifty-six thousand dollars. As a result, several articles discussing the debt were published in the *Religious Herald* in the hope they would stir up Southern Baptists to give more money to missions.

When Lottie finally received a copy of the paper by mail in Tengchow, she eagerly flipped it open. She soon wished she hadn't. She began to encounter the articles about the mission board's budget shortfall. One article noted, "Perhaps there are no people who watch the result of our campaign with more profound interest than our missionaries. If our people at home could realize what it means to the missionary when he feels that his brethren at home are not sustaining him...." And the editor wrote, "Our Boards must look to such restriction of their expenditures as will make such a stressful campaign as that which has just closed unnecessary."

A distressed Lottie quickly read between the lines. The Foreign Mission Board was not going to be able to send her any more money for famine relief, nor was it going to send any more missionaries to Tengchow until its finances had been put on a sure footing. To get through the hard times, Lottie and all the other Southern Baptist missionaries were going to have to tighten their belts until more money could be raised.

The needs of the local people, however, were great because of the continuing famine, and Lottie was unsure what to do. She had held out hope that the board would send out someone to help her in Tengchow, since there was still much work to be done there and in the surrounding area. Given the crisis, Lottie decided that every penny not spent on her was a penny she could give to help someone in need. Her old cook still made meals, but Lottie preferred to go out into the yard and give her portion of food to some passing emaciated child rather than eat it herself. Slowly, and without anyone realizing it, Lottie Moon was beginning to starve herself so that she could feed others.

By the time one of her fellow missionaries noticed what she was doing, Lottie weighed only fifty pounds. As a result, she was immediately bundled off to Laichowfu to be cared for by Dr. Gaston and his wife. Dr. Gaston decided, after several weeks of constant nursing, that Lottie's only hope of getting strong again was to go back to the United States. Cynthia Miller, a missionary nurse, offered to take an early furlough to accompany Lottie back to America. Of course, Lottie did not want to leave. There was still so much to do. Lottie, however, was outvoted by the other missionaries, who were intent on saving the life of their old friend and mentor.

"Just lay down now, Miss Moon," said one of the young missionaries as he lifted Lottie onto the pillows that had been placed inside the shentze in which she would travel to the coast.

Lottie looked up at him, her eyes bright. "I will not lay down, young man, but I will lie down!" she exclaimed in her best schoolteacher voice.

On December 13, 1912, Lottie was carried aboard the *Manchuria,* which was bound for San Francisco via Japan. Back in the United States, arrangements had been made for her arrival. Margaret, her elder brother Isaac's widow, had agreed to look after Lottie. And one of Lottie's missionary friends who was already home on furlough would meet the ship in San Francisco and escort her on the train journey back to Virginia. Once Lottie was safely in bed in her cabin, Lottie's trunk, which had accompanied her on earlier journeys home, was placed at the foot of the bed. In fact, the trunk was empty. Lottie had given away everything she owned to needy Chinese people and had brought the trunk along only for appearances when she arrived in America.

The ship steamed across the Yellow Sea until the coast of Japan came into view. As the *Manchuria* traveled along the coastline of Kyushu and Shikoku Islands, Lottie grew weaker. She slept for long periods, and when she was awake, she sipped the grape juice that had been brought aboard especially for her. Lottie was hardly conscious when the ship put in at the port of Kobe to take on more coal and passengers.

As the coal was being loaded, Lottie woke up and began talking in a firm voice. "Jesus loves me. This I know, for the Bible tells me so. Little ones to Him belong. They are weak but He is strong! Do you know that song, Cynthia?" she asked.

Cynthia nodded her head. "Yes, you have taught that song to thousands of Chinese people, haven't you?" she replied.

Lottie smiled, and her eyes lit up. She asked Cynthia to sing the song for her.

That night, as the *Manchuria* weighed anchor and set out into the Pacific Ocean, Lottie woke up several times saying, "We are weak but He is strong." When morning came, she opened her eyes. Cynthia Miller was right at her side. Then with a supreme effort, Lottie raised her arms, her hands formed into fists in the traditional greeting of one Chinese friend to another. With that gesture, Charlotte Digges Moon expelled the air from her lungs and breathed no more. It was Christmas Eve, 1912.

Chapter 17

An Offering

When the captain of the *Manchuria* was informed of Lottie's death, he ordered the ship to put in at Yokohama. Lottie's body was taken ashore and cremated on December 26. Her ashes were placed in an urn and returned to Cynthia Miller, who continued on to the United States with Lottie's ashes and empty trunk. On January 29, 1913, the remains of Charlotte Digges Moon were laid to rest beside her brother Isaac in the Crewe cemetery in Virginia.

Back in Tengchow, when news arrived of Lottie's death, the entire city was shocked. A monument was raised in honor of the woman who had given her all to bring hope and new life to so many Chinese people. Engraved on the monument was the inscription, "The Tengchow church remembers forever."

That was not the end of the story, however. Had Lottie Moon survived the voyage back to the United States, she would have undoubtedly made an impact upon the Southern Baptists. She always had in the past, but in her death, she stirred the denomination as never before. Across the country, Southern Baptist churches held memorial services for her. The *Foreign Mission Journal* lauded her for her bravery and devotion in the face of danger, declaring Lottie to be the "best man among our missionaries."

Cynthia Miller wrote about Lottie's final journey and ended her account with the words, "It is infinitely touching that those who work hardest and make the most sacrifices for the Master should suffer because those in the homeland fail to give what is needed."

Articles written about Lottie's death challenged Southern Baptist churches in a new way. Men and women alike began to ask themselves whether they could have done more to help support Lottie and the other Baptist missionaries who serve around the world.

The answer to their question was a resounding yes. Congregations tried to make amends to Lottie. The women of Virginia erected a monument at her gravesite, while the Crewe Baptist Church commissioned a stained-glass window featuring Lottie standing tall, a torch in one hand and a Bible in the other. But everyone knew this was not the sort of tribute Lottie would have really wanted. There had to be something more they could do.

The answer came to a journalist, Agnes Osborne, as the annual Christmas Offering for Foreign Missions campaign was being prepared. Agnes wrote to the women of the missionary union suggesting that the Christmas offering for 1913 be collected in memory of Lottie Moon. The hope was that evoking Lottie's name would be enough to encourage people to give so that the enormous debt that had weighed so heavily on Lottie's mind could be cleared. That year a record $38,035 was raised toward clearing the Foreign Mission Board's debt.

In 1918 Annie Armstrong, a supporter and admirer of Lottie, made a simple suggestion. Why not rename the Woman's Missionary Union annual offering in honor of the one woman who had inspired so many people both in the United States and in China? Everyone agreed, and the tradition of the Lottie Moon Christmas Offering for Foreign Missions was born. Finally Lottie had a memorial she would have wanted, not one of stone or glass but one of action.

The annual Lottie Moon Christmas Offering has been collected every year since 1918. Not only has it raised a large amount of money for foreign missions work, but also it has caused countless children and young people to ask: Who was Lottie Moon, and why do we honor her every year? Upon hearing the answer to their questions, many have been called to follow in Lottie Moon's footsteps.

Bibliography

Allen, Catherine B. *The New Lottie Moon Story.* Woman's Missionary Union, 1997.

Estep, William R. *Whole Gospel Whole World: The Foreign Mission Board of the Southern Baptist Convention 1845–1995.* Broadman & Holman Publishers, 1994.

Rankin, Jerry and Don Rutledge. *A Journey of Faith and Sacrifice: Retracing the Steps of Lottie Moon.* Woman's Missionary Union, 1996.

About the Authors

Janet and Geoff Benge are a husband and wife writing team with more than thirty years of writing experience. Janet is a former elementary school teacher. Geoff holds a degree in history. Originally from New Zealand, the Benges spent ten years serving with Youth With A Mission. They have two daughters, Laura and Shannon, and an adopted son, Lito. They make their home in the Orlando, Florida, area.

Also from Janet and Geoff Benge…

More adventure-filled biographies for ages 10 to 100!

Christian Heroes: Then and Now

Gladys Aylward: The Adventure of a Lifetime • 978-1-57658-019-6
Nate Saint: On a Wing and a Prayer • 978-1-57658-017-2
Hudson Taylor: Deep in the Heart of China • 978-1-57658-016-5
Amy Carmichael: Rescuer of Precious Gems • 978-1-57658-018-9
Eric Liddell: Something Greater Than Gold • 978-1-57658-137-7
Corrie ten Boom: Keeper of the Angels' Den • 978-1-57658-136-0
William Carey: Obliged to Go • 978-1-57658-147-6
George Müller: Guardian of Bristol's Orphans • 978-1-57658-145-2
Jim Elliot: One Great Purpose • 978-1-57658-146-9
Mary Slessor: Forward into Calabar • 978-1-57658-148-3
David Livingstone: Africa's Trailblazer • 978-1-57658-153-7
Betty Greene: Wings to Serve • 978-1-57658-152-0
Adoniram Judson: Bound for Burma • 978-1-57658-161-2
Cameron Townsend: Good News in Every Language • 978-1-57658-164-3
Jonathan Goforth: An Open Door in China • 978-1-57658-174-2
Lottie Moon: Giving Her All for China • 978-1-57658-188-9
John Williams: Messenger of Peace • 978-1-57658-256-5
William Booth: Soup, Soap, and Salvation • 978-1-57658-258-9
Rowland Bingham: Into Africa's Interior • 978-1-57658-282-4
Ida Scudder: Healing Bodies, Touching Hearts • 978-1-57658-285-5
Wilfred Grenfell: Fisher of Men • 978-1-57658-292-3
Lillian Trasher: The Greatest Wonder in Egypt • 978-1-57658-305-0
Loren Cunningham: Into All the World • 978-1-57658-199-5
Florence Young: Mission Accomplished • 978-1-57658-313-5
Sundar Singh: Footprints Over the Mountains • 978-1-57658-318-0
C.T. Studd: No Retreat • 978-1-57658-288-6
Rachel Saint: A Star in the Jungle • 978-1-57658-337-1
Brother Andrew: God's Secret Agent • 978-1-57658-355-5
Clarence Jones: Mr. Radio • 978-1-57658-343-2
Count Zinzendorf: Firstfruit • 978-1-57658-262-6
John Wesley: The World His Parish • 978-1-57658-382-1
C. S. Lewis: Master Storyteller • 978-1-57658-385-2
David Bussau: Facing the World Head-on • 978-1-57658-415-6
Jacob DeShazer: Forgive Your Enemies • 978-1-57658-475-0
Isobel Kuhn: On the Roof of the World • 978-1-57658-497-2
Elisabeth Elliot: Joyful Surrender • 978-1-57658-513-9
D. L. Moody: Bringing Souls to Christ • 978-1-57658-552-8
Paul Brand: Helping Hands • 978-1-57658-536-8
Dietrich Bonhoeffer: In the Midst of Wickedness • 978-1-57658-713-3
Francis Asbury: Circuit Rider • 978-1-57658-737-9
Samuel Zwemer: The Burden of Arabia • 978-1-57658-738-6

Klaus-Dieter John: Hope in the Land of the Incas • 978-1-57658-826-2
Mildred Cable: Through the Jade Gate • 978-1-57658-886-4
John Flynn: Into the Never Never • 978-1-57658-898-7
Richard Wurmbrand: Love Your Enemies • 978-1-57658-987-8
Charles Mulli: We Are Family • 978-1-57658-894-9
John Newton: Change of Heart • 978-1-57658-909-0
Helen Roseveare: Mama Luka • 978-1-57658-910-6
Norman Grubb: Mission Builder • 978-1-57658-915-1
Albert Schweitzer: Le Grand Docteur • 978-1-57658-961-8

Heroes of History

George Washington Carver: From Slave to Scientist • 978-1-883002-78-7
Abraham Lincoln: A New Birth of Freedom • 978-1-883002-79-4
Meriwether Lewis: Off the Edge of the Map • 978-1-883002-80-0
George Washington: True Patriot • 978-1-883002-81-7
William Penn: Liberty and Justice for All • 978-1-883002-82-4
Harriet Tubman: Freedombound • 978-1-883002-90-9
John Adams: Independence Forever • 978-1-883002-50-3
Clara Barton: Courage under Fire • 978-1-883002-51-0
Daniel Boone: Frontiersman • 978-1-932096-09-5
Theodore Roosevelt: An American Original • 978-1-932096-10-1
Douglas MacArthur: What Greater Honor • 978-1-932096-15-6
Benjamin Franklin: Live Wire • 978-1-932096-14-9
Christopher Columbus: Across the Ocean Sea • 978-1-932096-23-1
Laura Ingalls Wilder: A Storybook Life • 978-1-932096-32-3
Orville Wright: The Flyer • 978-1-932096-34-7
Captain John Smith: A Foothold in the New World • 978-1-932096-36-1
Thomas Edison: Inspiration and Hard Work • 978-1-932096-37-8
Alan Shepard: Higher and Faster • 978-1-932096-41-5
Ronald Reagan: Destiny at His Side • 978-1-932096-65-1
Davy Crockett: Ever Westward • 978-1-932096-67-5
Milton Hershey: More Than Chocolate • 978-1-932096-82-8
Billy Graham: America's Pastor • 978-1-62486-024-9
Ben Carson: A Chance at Life • 978-1-62486-034-8
Louis Zamperini: Redemption • 978-1-62486-049-2
Elizabeth Fry: Angel of Newgate • 978-1-62486-064-5
William Wilberforce: Take Up the Fight • 978-1-62486-057-7
William Bradford: Plymouth's Rock • 978-1-62486-092-8
Ernest Shackleton: Going South • 978-1-62486-093-5
Benjamin Rush: The Common Good • 978-1-62486-123-9
Dwight Eisenhower: Supreme Commander • 978-1-62486-142-0
Frederick Douglass: The Right to Dignity • 978-1-62486-151-2
Winston Churchill: Resolute • 978-1-62486-153-6

CHRISTIAN HEROES: THEN & NOW are available in paperback, e-book, and audiobook formats, with more coming soon!

www.YWAMpublishing.com